PASSIONATE
SPIRITUALITY

PASSIONATE SPIRITUALITY

Hildegard of Bingen
and
Hadewijch of Brabant

Elizabeth A. Dreyer

Paulist Press
New York / Mahwah, N.J.

Cover design by Stefan Killen Design Ltd.
Cover art: Scala/Art Resource, NY
Book design by Lynn Else

Library of Congress Cataloging-in-Publication Data

Dreyer, Elizabeth, 1945-
    Passionate spirituality : Hildegard of Bingen and Hadewijch of Brabant / Elizabeth A. Dreyer.
        p. cm.
    Includes bibliographical references and index.
    ISBN: 0-8091-4304-6 (alk. paper)
    1. Hildegard, Saint, 1098–1179. 2. Women mystics—Germany—History—To 1500. 3. Hadewijch, 13th cent. 4. Women mystics—Belgium—History—To 1500. 5. Love—Religious aspects—Christianity—History of doctrines—Middle Ages, 600–1500. 6. Spirituality—History—Middle Ages, 600–1500. I. Title.

    BV5077.G3D73 2005
    248.2'2'0922—dc22

                                                          2004024928

Published by Paulist Press
997 Macarthur Boulevard
Mahwah, New Jersey 07430

www.paulistpress.com

Printed and bound in the United States of America

Contents

Contents

For my sisters Kathleen, Mary Janet, and Virginia

Preface

Since publication of my Madeleva Lecture, *Passionate Women: Two Medieval Mystics*, almost fifteen years ago, I have continued to read about and reflect upon the theme of passion in the spiritual life and to ask questions about the meaning and presence of intense emotional engagement in our lives and spiritual journeys. The topic of emotion has grown more and more popular among philosophers, ethicists, scientists, sociologists, and students of the fine arts, as well as theologians. I continue to see the mystics as models and teachers who can instruct us about the deep feelings that run beneath the surface of an often hectic and superficial existence.

After *Passionate Women* went out of print, I received a steady stream of inquiries from laity, religious, and university, college, and seminary teachers about how to obtain a copy of this book. My own library now houses only two copies. One is dog-eared, stained, with yellowing pages, that has been loaned often and miraculously returned in each case. The other, discovered in our basement in a box of my stepson's college books, is in mint condition because never opened!

These diverse factors have led me to write an expanded and significantly revised text that includes new information, insights, and applications—a renewed invitation to readers to consider one of the most neglected, yet important aspects of the spiritual life. Hildegard of Bingen may be known to many readers. Her brilliant mind and soaring spirit make her a challenging but rewarding subject. Readers may be less familiar with Hadewijch, but she is a "must" in any work on mystical passion. I am happy to introduce her to those who have not yet met her.

My efforts will have been worthwhile if this little book sends people to the original sources to relish their artistry at firsthand. I have included significant samplings of each woman's work in order to entice the reader to that end.

I thank the Louisville Institute, the Lilly Foundation, and Fairfield University for funding that allowed me a semester free of teaching to bring this project to completion. I am also grateful to Michael Blastic, Elizabeth Johns, Harriet Luckman, Frank Hannafey, and Mark Burrows whose careful reading helped me to write a clearer and more integral book. Above all, I am grateful to all those who have graced my life and borne witness to their various passions, intense engagements, and commitments to life and to God. In particular, I want to thank my husband, John Bennett, an indefatigable editor, without whom my life would be lukewarm in ways too numerous to mention.

Friends, family, mentors, colleagues, and millennia of godly seekers help me see that a holy passionate life is possible, that it is attractive, and in all ways worth desiring. Hearts and heads alive with holy passion remind us of our truest selves, make the common good better, and honor God with a roaring blaze or deep intense silence of praise and thanksgiving. Like the fourth-century desert hermits, the medieval mystics lure us—in our time, place, and circumstances—to become "all flame." It is my hope that what follows will arouse curiosity about our deep emotions by enlightening our minds, warming our hearts, and alleviating our fears and embarrassments about feeling and expressing passion in our lives.

Elizabeth A. Dreyer
Fairfield University
Fairfield, Connecticut
September 7, 2004

Introduction

The historical record is all too clear about ways in which spiritual energy and passion have been put to destructive ends. Spiritual enthusiasm run amok has fueled war, violence, and oppressions too numerous to count. But perhaps we have not paid enough attention to ways in which passion can enhance and enrich the spiritual life. Spiritual power has led human beings to intense encounters with Deity, extraordinary actions of heroic love, and an endless stream of simple, daily acts of goodness.[1]

This book explores the roots and meaning of passion in the Christian West, and examines how passion was expressed in the lives of two quite different medieval women mystics—Hildegard of Bingen (1098–1179) and Hadewijch of Brabant (mid-thirteenth century). I also ask how their passionate engagement with divinity might make a contribution to contemporary spirituality. Mystical texts are intended to bring about transformation, but they also contain a wealth of theological content.[2] Thus, they are an important resource for the task of articulating for our time a theological spirituality, and a theology that is alive with Spirit. The point of examining the affections, then, is not to ignore or denigrate reason but to probe anew how heart and head can work in harmony to enrich the faith of the Christian community. At its best, the ongoing conversion of the spiritual life is both heartfelt and intelligent.

A negative effect of post-Enlightenment culture and the deepening divorce between spirituality and theology has been a loss of genuine affection in both arenas. As theology followed the course of academic methodologies, it found less and less room for feeling, which then became unmoored from reason. But a correction is afoot, and we find ourselves once again awakened to the value of the emotions and the body that gives them tangible form. Holistic anthropologies reflect a longing for the whole of life to be included in understanding the spiritual journey. We crave a balance between the important distance and perspective provided by reason and the fervor and energy of passionate living.

In many cultures, the affections are linked with women. The dualisms embedded in Greek philosophy and inherited by the West tended to oppose spirit and body, head and heart, heaven and earth, man and woman. The first term of these binary categories remains the more highly valued. My intention in exploring mystical passion is not to reinforce the narrow, gender-specific link between the passions and female human beings. Indeed, one of the fruits of the feminist movement has been to recognize women's intellectual legacy and allow men to make affective contributions to the common good. Rather, my hope is to call attention to the depth and creativity of the affections in two women's encounter with the divine, to examine how they are harmonized with reason, and to revalorize the passions as an integral part of the spiritual life.

The larger category in which passion rests is love—the centerpiece of the Christian faith. Christians give God the name of Love, profess the Spirit as the bond of love between the first and second Persons of the Trinity, and claim that the ability to live the Christian life lies in the love God first offers us (1 John 4:7–12). Jesus invited his disciples to be his friends and loved them passionately to the end (John 15:14–15). Love has held a preeminent position among the three theological virtues as the gift that animates our communal life and endures for all eternity. Aquinas names love as the form of all the virtues because it is meant to pervade all our actions. Thomas O'Meara specifies love's role: "Love gives a special dynamic and orientation to justice, enflames mercy, makes prudence not calculating but wise. Love is the Spirit of Jesus and the gospel's law because love does not halt at ideas and words but touches directly what it loves."[3]

Beyond the theological aspects of love, we need also to consider its psychological contours. In our culture, psychology is the most prominent category through which we understand ourselves as human beings. Prompting us to understand the human person in holistic ways, psychology no longer views the capacities of the human person in segregated, compartmentalized spheres, but speaks of new connections and interdependencies. These psychological insights provide a fruitful resource for exploring the Christian spiritual life.

It may also be helpful at the outset to clarify the term *mysticism* and its relationship to the broader category of "spirituality." The term *spirituality* is elusive and described in so many ways that some despair of using the term in any meaningful way at all. Nevertheless, *spirituality* can point us to the practical, existential, daily expression of ultimate beliefs. It is what faith looks like in the dispositions, words, and actions of a life. Sociologist Meredith McGuire uses the term *lived religion* to point to the way ordinary people experience and practice religion in their everyday lives. It is the way they make sense of their world and how they link the "big" stories of a religious tradition with their own personal and communal stories. Lived religion, or spirituality, "is constituted by the practices by which people remember, share, enact, adapt, create and combine the stories out of which they live."[4]

Walter Principe brings further clarity to the term *spirituality* by distinguishing three levels of meaning.[5] The first level encompasses the personal, lived aspect of spirituality. On a second level, spiritual experience takes place, and is passed on, in groups. The primary group is the family, but spiritual experience is also housed in parishes, or specialized groups such as Latin or Eastern; Methodist, Congregationalist, Lutheran or Unitarian;

religious orders such as Franciscans or Carmelites; or lay confra-
ternities such as Third Orders or cursillo. The third level
encompasses the formal study of spirituality. On this level,
scholars reflect on and analyze evidence from the first two levels in an organized and systematic fashion, devise categories and
criteria for evaluation, and employ disciplines such as anthropology, sociology, or psychology to shed light on the task.

For Christians, spirituality is understood in the context of a
trinitarian God who creates, redeems, and sanctifies humanity in
the context of a community—the People of God. By naming all
aspects of life as potentially infused by the Spirit, we acknowledge that spirituality embraces all aspects of the person—body,
mind, spirit—and all dimensions of existence—family, sexuality,
business, politics, education, media, the earth, and so on.
Christian spirituality is imbued with a sacramental consciousness that notices the presence of God in and through all of creation.

Within the larger category of spirituality, the term *mysticism*
describes those relationships with God that are characterized by
intensity and intimacy, and that "catch up" persons in their
entirety. The connections between mysticism and spirituality
are complex and important.[6] Like spirituality, definitions of mysticism are abundant and fraught with difficulty. Bernard McGinn
discusses the mystical element of religion as a way of life, the
part of Christian belief and practice "that concerns preparation
for, the consciousness of, and the reaction to what can be
described as the immediate or direct presence of God."[7] Joan
Mueller offers a simple description of mysticism as "a love affair
that demands looking at the other, both in the needs of our
neighbor and in prayer, and being concerned simply with the
other."[8] Mysticism is one aspect of a religious attitude within
which an intense relationship between a devout person and a
transcendent absolute becomes manifest. Mysticism does not
relegate morality or more ordinary spiritual expressions to a

lesser realm, but supports them, and indeed from one point of view constitutes their foundation.

In the last half of the twentieth century, scholars articulated a broader understanding of mysticism. Of particular note is German Jesuit Karl Rahner, whose theology had a significant impact on Vatican II.[9] Vatican II's emphasis on the universal call to holiness and on the foundational role of baptism in that call has caused the community to think about mysticism in new, more inclusive ways.[10] The basis for this understanding of mysticism is God's universal revelation of God's Self and the free human response to this loving communication and presence.

Some maintain that by its very nature, mysticism is excessive and outside the mainstream of societies and cultures, but I think such a description applies only to a few expressions of mysticism.[11] With Rahner, I suggest that extraordinary phenomena associated with mysticism—such as visions, locutions, and clairvoyance—need to be understood in their specific historical context and attributed to psychological elements that do not pertain to the essence of mystical experience. Most Christian mystics themselves insist that the psychological manifestations accompanying mystical experience be seen as secondary and accidental, rather than as constitutive markers of mystical experience. A broader, more capacious understanding of mysticism allows for a "mysticism of everyday life" that extends beyond monastic settings. But all forms of genuine Christian mysticism are marked by one form of excess—love.

Mysticism has also been described as "divinely inspired knowledge of divine truth."[12] This definition has the advantage of bringing the rational and the affective elements of mysticism together, for it points to how authentic experience of God—verbal, intellectual, affective, or ecstatic—yields a kind of knowing. One might even say that the "unknowing" of mystical experience results paradoxically in fresh knowledge of God's presence. This kind of full, rich, and broad knowledge of God includes, but need not be limited to, the extraordinary. Andrew Weeks acknowledges the diverse forms of mystical knowledge: "The divine knowledge may elude every positive formulation, or it may be knowledge of the quotidian things of our world—which are recognized in their essential being in God."[13]

In what follows, I offer some methodological cautions about how to retrieve medieval mystical material intelligently, and suggest themes in these texts that can be of particular relevance to contemporary spirituality. In chapter 2, I trace the roots of our understanding of the affections and passion in Greek culture, and identify ways in which the emotions have been neglected and devalued because of excessive emphasis on reason. This is followed by a closer look at the relationship between emotion and reason and the ways in which passion and the Christian life can be linked. I also examine biblical sources for the imagery and language of passionate love, with particular attention to the Song of Songs. This love poetry provides much of the language and imagery for certain strains of medieval mystical expression. This overview of various salient aspects of passion serves as the groundwork for chapters 3 and 4—two case studies that examine the presence of passion in the lives and writings of two very different medieval women mystics—Hildegard of Bingen, a Benedictine abbess who lived in the twelfth century, and Hadewijch of Brabant, a beguine from the thirteenth.[14] To conclude, I return to the present and suggest ways in which this journey into the meaning of passion in medieval mysticism can enliven contemporary quests for union with God.

Medieval women mystics use erotic, passionate language to describe their experiences of God, but when they do, they appear free and unselfconscious about it. In part, this is because they are speaking about *spiritual*, not physical love. Nevertheless, their fresh and energetic language provides an important resource for the recovery of a spirituality and theology that acknowledges the deep wells of feeling of which human beings are capable—in all aspects of our lives. They also reveal how to express these emotions in poetic, expressive language intended to move and compel others to love of God. By highlighting the intensely affective quality of this writing, I suggest that medieval women mystics provide a model for living the spiritual life that not only overcomes the bifurcation of affect and intellect, but celebrates the affections in productive and life-giving ways.[15] Spiritualities and theologies that are visibly born of the heart as well as the head quicken the spirit and offer a fuller account of the complex fullness of the human experience of God.

Chapter 1

Medieval Women Mystics:
Weird or Wonderful?

*Plus ça change, plus c'est la même chose. From the earliest years
of Christianity, the Church has had a problem with women.*

Barbara Newman[1]

Religious Women and Contemporary Scholarship

Once we are convinced of the wisdom of retrieving the tradition, the next question is how to do it. We begin by discussing several key methodological issues that are central to the responsible retrieval of the writings of medieval women mystics. I will then suggest four specific dimensions of this material that can contribute in helpful ways both to the contemporary practice of spirituality and to theological expression.

In the recent past, the number of books and articles on medieval women has dramatically increased. In large measure, this increase is the fruit of feminist scholars' desire to retrieve information about women from all historical periods. Initially, feminist scholars ignored ecclesial women, dismissing them as part of the problem rather than as a resource for a solution to women's oppression. In her book on Teresa of Avila, Carole Slade recalls that many feminist critics, focusing on the misogynist aspects of religious doctrine, dismissed religion altogether as a source of autonomy for women.[2] But this ideological stance is giving way to new questions and a new openness. In her comprehensive study, *The Creation of Feminist Consciousness*, historian Gerda Lerner describes her discovery of the significance of religion for women. She writes, "The insight that religion was the primary arena in which women fought for hundreds of years for feminist consciousness was not one I had previously had."[3] And in a volume on women in medieval history and historiography, Susan Mosher Stuard acknowledges the significant contributions that monastic women made to European culture.[4]

3

Grace Jantzen agrees and wonders if it is time to rethink, rather than simply reject or defend religion—given that it affects millions of women whether they are believers or not.[5] It is now common for scholars to study religion under the rubric of power, an especially relevant theme for women who have been marginalized by religion. Throughout history, religion (like most institutions) has functioned not only to liberate but also to oppress, and every generation must revisit the question about which aspects of the tradition are valuable and which harmful to women's well–being. What seemed liberating for one group in one period of history can be seen as oppressive in another, and vice versa. The skill of discernment—the art of distinguishing good from evil—is never absolute, but always open to discussion and argument. In the case of women and religion, how does one steer a course between defenders of religion who, happy with a secondary role for women, want to maintain the status quo, and those who want to discredit religion altogether? The first stance lacks honest, critical reflection (religion can do no wrong); the second smacks of reductionism and arrogance (religion has no redeeming features).

Continental philosopher Luce Irigaray offers a minimalist nod to religion: "It seems we are unable to eliminate or suppress the phenomenon of religion. It re–emerges in different forms, some of them perverse: sectarianism, theoretical or political dogmatism, religiosity.... Therefore, it is crucial that we rethink religion, and especially religious structures, categories, initiations, rules and utopias, all of which have been masculine for centuries."[6] Fortunately, motives for seeking fresh, more inclusive forms of religion go beyond Irigaray's view that scholarship on religion is a last resort, engaged only when efforts at elimination have failed.

Jantzen is more positive, observing that religion has been put at the service not only of repression, but also of reversal—toward justice, integrity, and love. But while forces for repression and liberation cannot be assigned to neat, generalized gender categories, the balance of power in religion has been overwhelmingly weighted toward men. Although Jantzen acknowledges the difficulty of dismantling patriarchy—given that women's hopes, dreams, and desires have been deeply molded by the very religions that need to be rethought—she identifies the works of medieval religious women as "discourses of reversal" that offer potential alternative ways to think about both religion and theological discourse.[7]

Other scholars are interested in literary and linguistic questions. What information can be gleaned from applying new methods and hermeneutic strategies to medieval texts? Some texts are of particular interest because they are among the first to be written in the vernacular. In this category, one can place the texts of the tenth–century Saxon canoness Hrosvit of Gandersheim; the thirteenth–century Flemish mystic Hadewijch of Brabant; the fourteenth–century English anchoress Julian of Norwich; and the fourteenth–century Italian saint Catherine of Siena.

Still other scholars, prompted by the work of feminist historians, are interested in recovering the lost or obscured history of women. These may be Jewish, Christian, Hindu, or Muslim women from all periods in history and all points of the globe. We simply want to know more about the religious dimensions of our female ancestors—who they were; what they thought, wrote, and accomplished; what they might have to say to us in the twenty–first century. The study of this history can offer perspective, insight, and comparative principles of judgment in the face of today's spiritual challenges.

The largest group drawn to women's religious history is composed of women engaged in an intentional spiritual life. These seekers turn to many sources for spiritual wisdom, often giving a prominent place to medieval women. There is also high interest in women of the Bible, women in the desert tradition, as well as contemporary figures such as Dorothy Day,

Simone Weil, and Bernadette Roberts. As I meet and talk with audiences across and beyond the United States, I am amazed at the significant number of Christians who for years have read, absorbed, and been enlivened by the texts of Christian medieval women mystics. Names once obscure to all but a small number of specialists have become household words for many—Hildegard of Bingen, Elisabeth of Schönau, Hadewijch of Brabant, Beatrice of Nazareth, Gertrude the Great, Angela of Foligno, Marguerite Porete, Birgitta of Sweden, and Julian of Norwich. And the more familiar stand–bys such as Heloise, Clare of Assisi, Catherine of Siena, and Teresa of Avila are even more widely read and appreciated.

Some might criticize the choice of medieval women mystics as elitist. The women who were educated enough to express themselves in a sophisticated way and either write or dictate their words to others are overwhelmingly from the upper classes. For the most part, wealth and position were prerequisites for entrance into monasteries. And women had to have some developed sense of themselves in order to write, speak, and act in public or private settings. We can respond to this criticism on two fronts. First, we simply do not have written evidence from "ordinary women," and other kinds of material evidence are often slim. Working with the texts we do have is better than ignoring them—leaving us with no female voice from the past at all. Second, I suggest that only rarely is evidence from any cohort in a population unreflective of currents in the wider culture. While the perspectives of rich, poor, and merchant class vary, all live in the same society and are influenced by and express its dynamics in some fashion. While class must be taken into consideration as a limiting factor, texts written in a milieu of wealth and influence can yield insights about the broader historical context and the role of women in church and society. Recent developments that view mysticism as grounded in baptism, and as a natural flowering of the Christian life, create a context for reception of this material that is quite different from that of the Middle Ages. Today, many "ordinary" Christians derive great spiritual benefit from reading and praying with these mystical texts.

This chapter addresses two issues. It begins with comments on method and context—I note the kinds of texts that have survived, call attention to some problems encountered in ascertaining authorship, sketch aspects of medieval culture that affected women's writing, and offer some caution about how to retrieve this material in a responsible, critical, and productive fashion. Second, I suggest four general areas in which medieval women can contribute to contemporary spiritual and theological concerns: (1) fidelity to experience; (2) a strong sense of the humanity of Christ; (3) joyful hope in the face of difficulties; and (4) liveliness of the affections.

Method and Context

Awareness of the ages–long marginalization of women in Christianity grows steadily. But many are still unaware of the ways in which our ideas about God, the human person, and the moral and spiritual life have been formed almost exclusively out of male experience—making the recovery of women's literature imperative. One can only lament the small number of Christian writings authored by women. The reasons for the paucity and obscurity of texts are many. Women in the past lacked education, time, and patronage (that is, money). Virginia Woolf's plea for a room of one's own seems, *mutatis mutandis*, relevant across the centuries. Social restrictions led all but the most intrepid of women to eschew writing in any form. And even when they did write, their texts were often ignored. For example, in the fourteen–volume *Cambridge History of English Literature*, Julian of Norwich is allotted only one short paragraph and Margery Kempe is not mentioned at all.[8] In spite of these obstacles, a significant number of texts from a variety of historical periods have survived and are now widely read.[9]

We have accounts of several women martyrs,[10] the best known of which is the *Passion of Sts. Perpetua and Felicitas,* dating from the year 202–203 in Carthage in North Africa.[11] This first-hand account is the earliest surviving text by a Christian woman. It is a marvelous text describing four dreams through which Perpetua, thrown in prison with her newborn child because of her conversion to Christianity, readies herself to leave conventional roles, ties, and commitments of daughter, sister, and mother to embrace physical death with its promise of eternal life. From the ninth century (841–843), we have a religious *Manual* written by a woman named Dhuoda, an educated laywoman living in southern France. The text is a moral guidebook written for her son, William.[12] Dhuoda counsels her son to lead a life of virtue based on the beatitudes and the gifts of the Holy Spirit. From the tenth century, we have the work of a Saxon canoness, Hrosvit of Gandersheim, considered to be the first known woman dramatist of Christianity, the first Saxon poet, and the first woman historian of Germany.[13] She expounds the glories of the Christian faith and the inevitable triumph of Christian over pagan ideals. In the twelfth century, there was a marked increase in literature by and about women—much of it emerging from the religious sphere of society—that would continue throughout the Middle Ages and beyond. Sources include pilgrimage diaries, hagiography, accounts of canonization processes, rules for religious communities, letters, prayers, and many accounts of religious experience.

Textual Issues

Most medieval manuscripts present a host of textual problems. In addition to finding, dating, and deciphering manuscripts, scholars must struggle to ascertain authorship. The modern idea that books are written by individuals who intend to produce a work of literature for which they are solely responsible would take medieval authors by surprise. In the Middle Ages, reading and writing were public acts. Most books were dictated orally to scribes and subsequently copied by hand. Editors often felt free to "improve" a text's accuracy or style in order to communicate more effectively to an intended audience, or protect the writer from censure. Translation from one language to another and copying errors by sleepy or blurry–eyed scribes further altered texts. For all these reasons, producing written texts was a joint effort, often involving several people. Shared authorship was often necessary in the case of women because they lacked formal education. Where we have multiple versions of a text, we see that differences between one rendition and another can be significant, making questions of authorship and authenticity challenging indeed.

This joint authorship is a prominent consideration in the texts of Elisabeth of Schönau and Margery Kempe, and in a lesser way, in the work of Hildegard of Bingen, Mechtild of Magdeburg, and Catherine of Siena.[14] Without access to formal education, women "wrote" under a variety of circumstances. When we are fairly certain that the text was written by the woman herself, the interpretive task is often complicated by her lack of attention to grammatical rules or eloquence of style. This can be true of texts written either in Latin or in the vernacular. Sometimes the scribes were men who were dedicated admirers and followers of the women for whom they wrote, and committed to represent the women's words carefully and accurately.

Initially, Hildegard of Bingen had both male and female scribes, who tell us they strove to be exacting in recording Hildegard's ideas. After their deaths, they were replaced by a theologian cleric who, according to Hildegard, took more liberties with the text. In one passage, we read a rather severe warning for anyone who might be tempted to tamper with her words after her death. She writes, "But whoever rashly conceals these words written by the finger of God, madly abridging them, or for any human reason taking them to a strange place and scoffing at them, let him be reprobate; and the finger of God shall crush him."[15] These are not the words of a shy, retiring woman. But there were also benefits to having a male theologian–editor change an infelicitous phrase inasmuch as it could save a woman from possible censure, imprisonment, or even death by civil or ecclesial authorities. Eckbert of Schönau, Elisabeth's brother, was very involved in her writing, and the famous sixteenth–century Spanish Carmelite Teresa of Avila had help from her friend Gratian and other influential clergy to help her avoid censure by the Inquisition.

A great deal of detective work is required to determine the level of influence of the scribe or editor.[16] Is the text likely to represent the ideas of a given female author a lot, somewhat, or in a few cases, almost not at all? We must remember that what today we would call "doctoring" a text was a common and accepted role for medieval scribes, who inevitably thought that they could say it better. Scholars work to identify and explain emendations to a text. In some cases, we can compare the texts written by the woman herself with those written about her by a male colleague. Male authors tended to romanticize or sentimentalize female virtues, highlight spectacular, dramatic acts, and use erotic imagery in ways different from the female mystics' accounts of their own experience. Men were also far more likely to attribute sexual or bodily temptation to female nature and to imagine women struggling to overcome the flesh.[17] John Anson argues that the common story of the woman who masquerades as a man in order to enter a monastery appears to reflect male anxiety more frequently than it does historical reality.[18]

Medieval Writing

It is difficult for us to imagine the transgression involved when a medieval woman chose to write for a public audience. In most cases, the point of entering a medieval monastery was to withdraw from the world in order to focus on God.[19] Thus, writing and speaking publicly was seen as a transgression, if not a betrayal, of that vocation. This tension is visible in the writing of male as well as female monastics, even though being male, educated, and sometimes ordained, provided a more acceptable platform from which to speak and teach about God.

Bernard of Clairvaux, an influential figure in twelfth–century Europe, constantly struggled with this tension. He had joined the monastery to retreat from the world, and yet found himself in the realm of princes, bishops, kings, and popes, preaching Crusades, and often asked to intervene in affairs of church and state. His high interest in the virtue of humility suggests a life-long inner struggle between what he professed as a Cistercian monk and what turned out to be the reality of his life. A twentieth–century analogue is Thomas Merton, Trappist monk and leading author, who tells the famous story of his journey into Louisville to take the oath of citizenship after he had become a monk. There was a room full of persons taking the oath that day, but the rows and rows of media—television cameras, radio microphones, and spotlights—were there not for the forty or so anonymous new Americans but for him, the one who had chosen to be silent and invisible.

In the case of medieval women, the boldness required to write or teach in public was extraordinary. It is difficult to find a contemporary analogue to help us understand the risks involved when a medieval woman chose to write for an audience beyond her convent or monastery. In our society, writing is not only taken for granted but is in such abundance that it threatens to overwhelm us. Women are more and more part of the literate world—from university classrooms, to politics, journalism, and entertainment. In the Middle Ages, it was not only that social and ecclesial authorities might disapprove, threaten, or levy punishments when women wrote, but also the women themselves would have interiorized these taboos. Thus their struggle was both exterior and interior, and one has the sense that the interior battle may have been the more fierce.

Bernard McGinn cites one example of how a medieval theologian dealt with the growing presence of women as "players" in the church in the thirteenth century. Around 1290, Henry of Ghent, a noted theologian at the University of Paris, raised this question: "Whether a woman can be a doctor of theology?" In his response, he makes a distinction. While "women cannot officially (*ex officio*) serve as doctors of theology, because they cannot possess the four public marks of doctoral status (constancy, efficacy, authority, and effect)," it is well known that they can teach from "divine favor (*ex beneficio*) and the fervor of charity if they possess sound doctrine."[20] In the next chapter, we explore this idea of fervor (what I am calling passion), which was both a hallmark of the way women expressed their ideas about God and, when linked to love and the Spirit, a justifying and validating characteristic that legitimated their speech. Significant advances have occurred in giving voice to women's theological ideas, but in many arenas women are still like Henry of Ghent— compelled to devise "creative bypasses" so that the theological and spiritual wisdom of women might be heard by all.

We can get some sense of the risk in transgressing conventions when we think of women today who venture into new roles in science or government, business, the military, or the church. Think of the reactions of some in our own time to even the *thought* of a female president, a female minister, priest, or bishop; a female general, or even an active first lady. And we continue to see women across the globe risk exile and even death for their beliefs and convictions. We witness the high public price these women pay, not to mention the inner struggles that such women no doubt experience as they choose to "step out of line." Our own experience of these pioneering women gives us some small glimpse into what was at stake and the price a medieval woman religious might pay to teach or write in public.

When we read that a medieval woman resisted writing, or had doubts about her ability to write, or wrote only when commanded by a superior or male spiritual director, we need to understand the context in which this reluctance occurred if we are to get a truer sense of its meaning. Often one of the best arguments used to get a woman to write was that other women religious or Christian faithful needed help in exploring relationships with God from someone who knew the terrain and was good at describing it. The motive of service to others could mitigate a woman's sense that she was over–stepping the boundaries of what was "appropriate."

Critical Correlation

For many, the point of attending to medieval mystical material critically and carefully is to see if there are ways it can be brought forward into our own time. Initial exposure to these texts may cause the uninitiated reader to wonder about the sanity of those drawn to them. Their diversity is indeed challenging and some of their attitudes, convictions, language, imagery, and religious practices are daunting if not downright repulsive. The social, ecclesial, intellectual, and cultural world of the Middle Ages could not be more foreign to our own. We call to mind Hobbes's (1588–1679) dismissive quip, that life is "nasty, brutish and short"! Women had neither the political nor the economic rights we enjoy today. None had access to formal university education. And their interest in the graphic depiction of the Crucified, extreme forms of asceticism, illness often unto death, and erotic, nuptial, mystical themes seem odd indeed to contemporary people.[21]

Carol Lee Flinders presses feminists to reexamine distancing strategies, such as labeling medieval women mystics as weird or pathological, that have kept women today from taking them seriously. She fears that this negative approach may keep some women from their own full unfolding, and she advocates study of women like Julian of Norwich and Teresa of Avila in order to learn from their religious disciplines.[22] But though our ultimate aim is critical retrieval of this material for spiritual and theological purposes, it is important to underline that many aspects of medieval women's spirituality are justly judged irrelevant and even harmful for persons today. In the Epilogue of *Holy Feast, Holy Fast*, medieval historian Caroline Walker Bynum reminds us that the "practices and symbols of any culture are so embedded in that culture as to be inseparable from it... [The symbols, behaviors, and doctrines of the Middle Ages were] produced in a world that has vanished."[23] She states quite bluntly, "Those recent scholars who have attempted to urge medieval devotions on the modern church run the risk of ignoring the savagery of some medieval asceticism, the sentimentality of much medieval preaching, the sexism of medieval society." In fact, she rightly cautions against making facile connections in either direction between the Middle Ages and the present.[24]

For example, readers encounter stories in which Catherine of Siena drank pus, Catherine of Genoa ate lice, and Angela of Foligno drank the water with which the sores of lepers had been bathed. Lutgard of Aywières was picked up by Christ on the cross so that she could nurse at his side. In the search to understand such behaviors, scholars posit a link with medieval women's desire to imitate the suffering Christ. Through these dramatic gestures, "they ate and drank the suffering of Christ and of their fellow creatures."[25] Thus, these gestures are interpreted as signs of relationship with Christ and service to others. The night after her experience of drinking the pus of a sick woman for whom she was caring, Catherine of Siena reports a vision in which God says to her, "Previously you had renounced all that the body takes pleasure in....But yesterday the intensity of your ardent love for me overcame even the instinctive reflexes of your body itself....So I today shall give you a drink that transcends in perfection any that human nature can provide." Christ then invites Catherine to drink from the wound in his side.[26] In a letter to a Florentine abbess, Catherine writes, "We cannot nourish others unless we nourish ourselves at the breasts of divine charity."[27] Bynum writes, "to eat to Catherine means *to be* or *to become, to take in* or *to love*."[28]

It is not possible here to examine the nuances of context and meaning of each of the incidents mentioned above, but I can offer a few general comments. Many of these women put their own distinctive mark on the broader tendency of the Middle Ages to focus on the human, rather than on the divine Jesus, and in particular on the suffering endured by Jesus on the cross. This emphasis is further documented in medieval art and preaching, and is often associated with the spiritual genius of Francis of Assisi, whose story includes being marked in his own body with the signs of Jesus' crucifixion. And Francis has his own story of how kissing a leper symbolized a major conversion in his life.[29]

In fourteenth–century England, Julian of Norwich offers an example of a graphic description of the Passion:

> And after this, as I watched, I saw the body bleeding copiously in representation of the scourging...the fair skin was deeply broken into the tender flesh through the vicious blows delivered all over the lovely body. The hot blood ran out so plentifully that neither skin nor wounds could be seen, but everything seemed to be blood.[30]

The women share quite literally in Christ's Passion. In late thirteenth–century Italy, lay Franciscan Angela of Foligno's scribe describes her torment.

> Christ's faithful one told me, brother scribe, that she thought that the bodily ailments she endured were

beyond description, and the ailments and sufferings of her soul were even more beyond any kind of comparison. In short, concerning the sufferings of the body, I heard her say that there was not one part of her body which had not suffered horribly.[31]

Carolyn Walker Bynum explains, "In a fierce imitation of the cross that included self–flagellation, self–starvation, and acute illness, women became the macerated body of the Savior."[32] The medieval notion of the imitation of Christ involved a fusion with the suffering physicality of Christ.[33]

A few scholars suggest that such extreme ascetical behavior suggests an interiorization of medieval society's disregard for women, resulting in expressions of self–hate and self–destruction. Others, more accurately, I think, choose to examine these extreme forms of behavior in a much wider social, ecclesial context. They suggest that for many medieval women religious, to suffer was to save and be saved. Suffering was linked with spiritual fertility and generativity. Severe ascetic practice was aimed at killing self–will, joining one's will to that of Christ. Bynum concludes that the "extreme asceticism and literalism of these women's spirituality were not, at the deepest level, masochism or dualism but, rather, efforts to gain power and to give meaning."[34] It is obvious that most of these women had unusually strong self–concepts, healthy egos, and the ability to accomplish significant work for church and society due to their strong personalities and intense religious commitments.

Other students of these texts explore the meaning of prominent symbols and metaphors, such as blood, precious stones, and various kinds of architectural images. Yet others explore these texts with questions about power, vested interests, and social and ecclesial manipulation. How did the visions and writings of medieval women help them achieve power and influence in a society that denied them both?[35]

Religious communities that revere these women as foundresses, heroines, and saints, and laywomen (and men) hungry to find female models of holiness are eager to learn about medieval women. However, such enthusiasm can cause the devotee to gloss over the unhelpful, distasteful, and potentially harmful dimensions of the spiritualities of many medieval women mystics. On one level, these texts call attention to themes of bodiliness, generativity, and nourishment that open out to embrace contemporary experience. But on another level, they are dangerous. Who would advocate self–starvation for themselves, spouses, children, or friends as a way to God? Who does not want to abandon the hate and prejudice of many in the medieval church against Jews and Muslims? And should medieval women mystics' repeated call to seek suffering be the central way in which twenty–first–century Christians understand the imitation of Christ?

And yet, in spite of these difficulties, many diverse groups of persons find a profound sense of connection with aspects of the theology, spirituality, and insight into the human psyche, represented in the works of these medieval women mystics.[36] What do contemporary fans of these women see in their lives and texts? Why do they seem to strike a chord with many who struggle to live creative spiritual lives today, in spite of the religious and cultural distance? And finally, how might the new, curious reader be helped to enter more fully into the depths of their thought?

Past Wisdom Speaks to the Present

Let us turn to our second consideration—what are some of the themes in this literature that can be of service to women and men on a postmodern quest for holiness? From a field of many possibilities, I identify four aspects of medieval women's accounts of their religious experience that may resonate with contemporary Christians seeking a more intentional spirituality: (1) the experiential base of their spirituality; (2) the focus on the human Christ; (3) hope and optimism in the face of difficulty; (4) their implicit invitation to be delivered from lukewarm affections.

Reliance on Experience

While women were barred from formal university study, families of means did have ways to educate daughters. In fact, many texts of medieval women mystics reflect a surprisingly high level of erudition. Hildegard of Bingen, Hadewijch of Brabant, and Julian of Norwich are prime examples. Young girls could be sent to study in monastic schools or under religious sisters in the local community.[37] Hildegard was sent at the age of eight to be tutored by Jutta von Spanheim, who lived in a small cloister near her home. And many know the story of Heloise, whose uncle hired Abelard as a tutor to educate her at home. At times, one is astonished at the level of theological sophistication manifest in many texts. They reveal women of obviously high intelligence who built on the education they did receive through contemplative reflection on scripture and tradition, and through conversation with their more formally learned male colleagues.

Without the university schooling that would have conditioned these women to use more settled philosophical and theological categories to speak of their religious experience, they are thrown back on that experience and forced to attend to it carefully in order to discern its meaning. As a result, one encounters freshness in the content, language, and imagery of these texts. For example, in the thirteenth–century text, *Spiritual Exercises*, Gertrude the Great personalizes the liturgy of profession—the ritual signaling her official reception into religious life—in ways that allow the reader, first, to become more conscious of the ways in which liturgical language has become

18

stilted and empty today, and second, to use her text as entry into a renewed understanding of, and participation in, baptismal life.[38]

In another example, Julian of Norwich's *Showings* contains one of the most masterful and convincing theologies of the Trinity in the tradition.[39] She is not ignorant of traditional trinitarian theology, but she does not rely on it at the expense of her experience of the Trinity in her revelations. In her visions, she encounters the intense, joyful, affective interrelationships within the Trinity, and she communicates this life with a rare directness and spontaneity. Julian is also known for attributing motherhood to Christ, and, by extension, to all three Persons of the Trinity. When her visions reveal aspects of sin that challenge emphases in the church's doctrine in the fourteenth century, she does not abandon her own truth, but struggles tenaciously to express it. And in sixteenth–century Spain, Teresa of Avila regularly disagrees with advice she is given by spiritual directors when it flies in the face of her experience. She laments having to work with clerical directors who, inexperienced in the spiritual life themselves, tend to get in the way rather than to help.[40]

While in some instances the mystics' insistence on the correctness of their positions could aptly be interpreted as egoism or plain stubbornness, one is more likely to be impressed by the courage of their convictions. Peter Dronke says of Hildegard of Bingen:

> Her approach to every problem—human, scientific, artistic, or theological—was her own. She took nothing ready–made. Her conviction that she *saw* the answers to the problems in her waking vision meant that she did not have to defer to established answers. Often we see she does not give a damn about these, however powerful their proponents. Many times she expresses herself courteously and modestly; yet when

19

it comes to asserting what she believes to be right, she will do it bravely, outfacing all opposition.[41]

These women *trusted* their experience and, in addition, remained faithful to it at great risk. We have noted that it was radically countercultural for women to take up the pen. It was not as though no one would know or care when they "went public" or when they questioned the inherited tradition. If their texts were intended to circulate only within their religious communities, they found a good deal of tolerance on the part of church leadership. But women who wrote or spoke publicly faced a different kind of scrutiny. In varying degrees, medieval women religious were suspect. Their very numbers and prominence in the medieval period brought forth suspicions grounded in a cultural misogynism.[42] Ecclesial authorities often saw women as dangerous, physically and intellectually weak, emotionally unstable and untrustworthy candidates for the higher reaches of the spiritual life. Many women suffered from ecclesiastical skepticism and oppression. They were interrogated by the Inquisition, and for some, the outcome was death. In 1310, in Paris, Marguerite Porete was burned at the stake as a heretic for her book *The Mirror of Simple Souls*. The three theologians to whom she had submitted her text had found no fault with it.[43]

We have noted the crucial advocacy role played by wealthy, influential men—relatives or clergy who knew and admired these women. One can mention a somewhat reluctant Bernard of Clairvaux for Hildegard of Bingen, the hermit Roger for Christina Markyate, Fra Arnaldo for Angela of Foligno, Raymond of Capua for Catherine of Siena, and Cardinal Cisneros for Teresa of Avila. But help from others does not diminish the courage and perseverance many of these women exhibited in the face of risk and at times serious danger. No matter the historical period, there is usually a price to pay for challenging the status quo or going public with a grievance.

Medieval women were no different. Their commitment to the truth as they saw it motivated them to struggle heroically to understand the depth and nuances of their revelations and to identify and employ any number of creative bypasses that enabled some to remain true to themselves and avoid oblivion, punishment, or extinction.

One also senses that these women were not immune from occasional, severe self–doubt, discouragement, and even what today we label "depression."[44] Their stories are not ethereal fairy tales, but accounts of real women, many of whom engaged in lifelong struggles against themselves and against forces in church and society aimed at limiting their power and their means of expression. One senses that the words of encourage- ment offered to their readers are also intended for themselves, cheering themselves on to perdure when the going got rough as it inevitably did. Such doubt is palpably visible in the texts of Hildegard, Julian, and Catherine of Siena.

What is the effect on the reader of this fidelity to experi- ence? To begin, we can see in these women's respect for their experience an enhancement of our own. They challenge us to stand tall, to take ourselves seriously, to appreciate more fully the legacy we share of being women of spirit. They invite Christian believers to attend with reverence to the ways in which God is operative in their lives, to trust in these ways, and to be emboldened to live them out in spite of obstacles and doubts. Second, we have to admire the courage of many of these women. They become sources of celebration and pride in the long, buried heritage of strong, holy, intelligent women—and models in a time when courage is often the order of the day. The bold commitment of a Hildegard or a Clare or a Teresa calls us to accountability to our own encounters with life and with God.

Finally, their fidelity to experience leads them to create a theology that is ineluctably bound to the existential reality of encounter with God. Their theology emerges not from an ivory tower but from the crucible of engaging the living God. We can also be grateful for the fresh and, at times, startling metaphors and images offered by these women. Often they are ones we have not heard before and can thus contribute to the ongoing renewal of theological language. Julian experiences herself wrapped "round by God" the way clothing and skin wraps and embraces her body.[45] Such imagery can help readers uncover lost truths of their experience; it provides a valuable complement to more traditional perspectives.

Emphasis on the Humanity of Christ

A second contribution of this material is its interest in the humanity of Christ—a theme to which we will return in subsequent chapters. In the twentieth century, theologians became more aware of the important role of history in the theological task, and of how historical consciousness influenced our understanding of Christ. We witnessed a turn from a "high" Christology, in which Christ is viewed primarily as the divine, pre–existent Son of God, to a "Christology from below" that emphasizes Christ's humanity, his Jewishness, and his choice to enter fully into the human condition as a poor first–century Nazarene.

This contemporary interest in the human Jesus is mirrored in distinctive ways in the spiritual writings of the medieval period. Imaging Christ in human terms also reinforced emphasis on the affections. Anselm of Canterbury (d. 1109) is a key figure in this turn. His *Prayers and Meditations* reveals a man who, in addition to being a rigorous scholar, imagines a human Jesus with whom he can express the warm, emotive side of his personality. Bernard of Clairvaux (d. 1153) captured aspects of his culture in a spirituality centered on an intense love of the human Christ as the bridegroom of the soul. Bernard transformed the erotic poetry of the courtly love tradition into a new key by using its language to express the deepest mysteries of mystical union. In chapter 4, we will see how Hadewijch continues this tradition a century later. Also in the twelfth century in England, Aelred of Rievaulx (d. 1167) wrote *On Spiritual Friendship*, a text that not only dignifies human friendship, but expands the biblical "God is love" to "God is friendship." Also implicit in the theology of the period was a turn from emphasis on atonement and final judgment to interest in creation and incarnation, a turn that also served to put the spotlight on the human Jesus.[46]

For all the beauty of this tradition, emphasis on affectivity always runs the risk of falling victim to sentimentality or excess. Devotions to the Sacred Heart and to the Body of Christ in the Eucharist involved popular practices that lent themselves to extreme as well as genuine expression. For example, medieval worshippers are known to have rushed from church to church to witness repeated elevations of the host at Eucharist.[47] A custom celebrating Christ's humanity that has perdured throughout the centuries in artistic imagery and popular piety is the veneration of the crèche associated with Francis of Assisi.

Medieval women mystics represent the apex of this tradition honoring the humanity of Christ. For many of them, the spiritual life was experienced primarily as relationship, understood preeminently as a relationship with Christ in his humanity. No longer distant and fearsome, Christ is associated with the human functions of mothering, nursing, lovemaking—thus becoming eminently familiar and approachable. For Gertrude of Helfta and Mechtild of Hackeborn, the humanity of Christ symbolizes our incorporation into divinity. Christ *is* what we are; our humanity is in Christ. It is not so much the spark of divinity in humans, but the containment of our humanity in Christ that affords us salvation.[48] In her *Spiritual Exercises* Gertrude says, "May all the efficacy and virtue of your divinity praise you for me; may all the friendship and affection of your humanity give satisfaction to you for me."[49] And further on in the same text: "Receive me, most loving Jesus, into your most gracious brotherliness; may you bear with me the burden of the day's heat; and may I have you as consolation for all my labor, as my partner on the road, as guide and companion."⁵⁰

Hadewijch of Brabant experienced Christ's humanity in dramatic ways. Her letters and visions are filled with references to her stormy and intimate love affair with a divine force she names "Love." In her first vision, she hears Christ say that if we want to identify with him in his humanity, we must desire to be poor, miserable, and despised. But because of love, all grief will taste sweeter than all earthly pleasures, and therefore we should not let suffering sadden us.⁵¹ Her "low" Christology is most evident in the following passage in which Christ says, "[N]ever for a single instant did I call upon my power to give myself relief when I was in need, and never did I seek to profit from the gifts of my Spirit, but I won them at the price of sufferings and through my Father....Never did I dispel my griefs or my pains with the aid of my omnipotence."⁵² And finally, one must mention the numerous lyrical passages in which Hadewijch describes her profoundly intimate relationship with Love as friend and lover—passages we will examine in more detail in chapter 4.

Many are familiar with the language Julian of Norwich employs when she speaks of Christ—"courteous giver," compassionate comforter, one who suffers in joy. For Julian, the human qualities of Christ are taken up into the very heart of the Trinity. She notes how astonished she is that "he who is so to be revered and feared would be so familiar with a sinful creature living in this wretched flesh."⁵³ We have already called attention to the ways in which Julian speaks of Christ as our clothing, wrapping us round in his love.⁵⁴ When we come to Jesus to ask for forgiveness, she says:

> ...our courteous Lord shows himself to the soul, happily and with the gladdest countenance, welcoming it

as a friend, as if it had been in pain and prison, saying: "My dear darling, I am glad that you have come to me in all your woe. I have always been with you, and now you see me loving, and we are made one in bliss."[55]

In one of her visions, Julian receives a suggestion to look away from the cross toward heaven. She replies that she cannot, for Christ is her heaven. She says she would rather have remained in "pain until Judgment Day than have come to heaven any other way than by him....So I was taught to choose Jesus for my heaven, whom I saw only in pain at that time. No other heaven was pleasing to me than Jesus, who will be my bliss when I am there."[56] Like others, Julian sees both the glory of the divinity and the "preciousness and tenderness" of Christ's body united with it.[57]

In the ninth chapter of her autobiography, Teresa of Avila describes her prayer as she began to awaken to Christ.

> As I could not reason with my mind, I would try to make pictures of Christ inwardly; and I used to think I felt better when I dwelt on those parts of His life when He was most often alone. It seemed to me that His being alone and afflicted, like a person in need, made it possible for me to approach Him....I was particularly attached to the prayer in the Garden, where I would go to keep Him company. I would think of the sweat and of the affliction He endured there. I wished I could have wiped that grievous sweat from His face, but I remember that I never dared to resolve to do so, for the gravity of my sins stood in the way.[58]

Later on, Teresa questions the theory of prayer that teaches that Christ's humanity can hinder or impede those who are advancing toward perfection. She says, "I cannot bear the idea that we must withdraw ourselves entirely from Christ and treat the divine body of his as though it were on a level with our miseries and with all created things."[59]

These women speak to us today because we too are drawn by the human Christ. In articulating their experience of Christ's humanity, they offer us language, images, and a variety of spaces in which to work out a relationship with Christ. They underscore ways in which human life is dignified and raised up in the humanity of Christ. And they find comfort in the intimate connection to divinity and redemption that Christ provides for us in his humanity. Medieval women mystics are not afraid to explore the range and depth of feeling as they relate to a human Christ. The infinite love and care shown by Christ in his humanity also emboldens them to speak out and act on behalf of other humans in a life dedicated to virtue. The royal Christ is tempered with images of "homely" approachability.

Heralds of Joyful Hope

After an encounter with texts replete with talk about fasting, blood, and suffering, many readers are amazed at the buoyant, hopeful feeling with which they are left. But in these texts, suffering is not for its own sake. These mystics experience suffering as a difficult, but joyful participation in the life of Christ, and they write powerfully of the creative aspects of this paradox. Hadewijch expresses this in one of her poems:

> What is sweetest in Love is her tempestuousness;
> Her deepest abyss is her most beautiful form;
> To lose one's way in her is to touch her close at hand;
> To die of hunger for her is to feed and taste;
> Her despair is assurance;
> Her sorest wounding is all curing;
> To waste away for her sake is to be in repose;
> Her sorest blow is her sweetest consolation;
> Her ruthless robbery is great profit;

Her withdrawal is approach;
Her deepest silence is her sublime song;
Her greatest wrath is her dearest thanks;
Her greatest threat is pure fidelity;
Her sadness is the alleviation of all pain.[60]

Suffering may be everywhere, but joy is never far behind and always has the last word.

In many of these texts, the women discover that the joy God experiences in bringing redemption far outweighs the suffering of the cross. The Lord says to Julian, "It is a joy, a bliss, an endless delight to me that ever I suffered my Passion for you; and if I could suffer more, I should suffer more."[61] This kind of suffering does not drag us down, but holds us up, and such accounts offer understanding and even the possibility of appreciating the suffering that life inevitably brings.

Another source of optimism in these texts is the portrayal of a positive and dynamic anthropology. Though God remains the exclusive source and eternal giver of grace, and the power of sin is never underestimated, it does not follow that the human person is merely an inept, stupid bumbler. While they grant that human dignity is conferred by God, these women have a profound sense of their own worth and glory—in spite of protestations of weakness and ignorance. In her *Mirror of Simple Souls*, Marguerite Porete articulates what she sees as the blessing of human evil:

God has nowhere to put his goodness, if not in me....
Now if I am all evil, and God is all goodness, and one must give alms to the poorest being, or else one takes away what is hers by right, and God can do no wrong ...then I am God's goodness, because of my neediness....So it is clearly evident that I am the praise of God forever, and the salvation of human creatures—

27

for the salvation of any creature is nothing but knowing the goodness of God.[62]

We encounter creative, competent, assured, self–confident
women who see not only themselves but the whole Christian
people as dignified. In chapter 22 of her *Revelations,* Julian says of
her "even–Christians": "We are God's bliss, God's reward. We are
God's honour and God's crown. And this was a singular wonder
and a most delectable contemplation, that we are God's
crown."[63] And in *The Interior Castle,* Teresa of Avila envisions a
God who carries on intimate conversations in the innermost
recesses of one's being.

The women personally exemplify their positive anthropology by trusting their own experience, even when it came into
conflict with official doctrinal positions. Hadewijch of Brabant,
Julian of Norwich, and Teresa of Avila contribute to the doctrine
of the incarnation by remaining faithful to their knowledge that
the humanity of Christ should never be left behind as one
advances in the spiritual life. Julian struggles with the contradictions between the way God and the church see sin. Without
arrogance, many of these women refuse to lay aside the truth of
their experience to avoid conflict. They inspire hope for people
who live in a world that often feels like a "vale of tears." Their
courage calls the reader to follow in their footsteps, that is, to
begin to trust the ways in which God is working, and to struggle to be faithful to that experience. The self–confidence of
these women inspires us to see ourselves as godly beings, dignified and worthy of respect.

Readers also feel hopeful because they feel included in the
embrace of these mystics. As we have seen, these women write,
sometimes against their own preference, in order that others
may benefit from their experience. They are clear that life with
God is not an exclusive club. They literally hunger for others to
follow the difficult but rewarding path of intimate relationship

with God. Most addressed an audience of religious and clergy, but we are right to extend their invitation to all others who desire holiness. The anchorite Julian casts her net in this way to all her "even–Christians."

These women are confident of their mission—and, as reformers, they can speak in extremely harsh and frank tones about abuse in the church. I offer one example from Hildegard of Bingen.

> But if priests do not show the people the authority of their office, they are not priests but ravenous wolves, for they hold their office by robbery as a wolf cruelly snatches a sheep, doing their own will instead of caring for the sheep. And, because they live perversely, they are afraid to teach true doctrine to the people; they consent to iniquity as to a lord, for they harbor carnal desires, and they close the door of their heart to a helper as if to a stranger; for justice is of God. (*Scivias* II.6.94)

Honesty about spiritual failure is necessary to genuine hope. But their criticism does not emerge out of an attitude of superiority, but rather out of authentic indignation, and from the margins. They do not "talk down to" or pretend to instruct their readers in a condescending way. Rather, they seem to have a genuine desire for holiness for the wider faith community, and in this desire, they dignify us, their readers. Their humble confidence and hope can be ours.

Finally, we can glean a sense of optimism from the intense, intimate, and mutual fidelity these women experience with God. Relational metaphors such as spouse, lover, mother, nurse, and friend give dynamism and variety to the divine–human relationship. These relationships are certainly not casual, nor are they one–sided. Whether overtly stated or simply implied, the

descriptions convince us that these love affairs—although difficult beyond imagining—are not soon going to pass away. It is
not just that the women are committed to be faithful, but God's
very Self is enmeshed in the relationship just as deeply as they
are. Julian says of Christ, "For he still has that same thirst and
longing which he had upon the Cross, which desire, longing
and thirst, as I see it, were in him from without beginning; and
he will have this until the time that the last soul which will be
saved has come up into his bliss."[64] In imagery reminiscent of the
Song of Songs, these women are enmeshed in a passionate relationship. And just as they experience a point at which it
becomes impossible to walk away from God, they know that
God has been at that point from all eternity. This God, who is
endless love, is not capable of walking away from creation.

Deliverance from Lukewarm Affections

Another welcome gift from these mystical texts is the invitation to rekindle emotions. In the fourth mansion of her *Interior
Castle*, Teresa says, "The soul experiences deep feelings when it
sees itself close to God."[65] And Julian: "That honourable city in
which our Lord Jesus sits is our sensuality, in which he is
enclosed."[66] In these mystical texts, feelings are not dulled or
suppressed. Rather, we are overwhelmed by the range and
intensity of expressed emotion. The list is extensive—longing,
release, joy, delight, contentment, agony, loneliness, jealousy,
tenderness, deprivation, pain, arousal, despair, ecstasy, compassion. If we accept Rosemary Haughton's definition of passion as
the drive of powerful emotion toward the knowledge, and, in
some sense, the possession of an object outside oneself,[67] we
can describe medieval women mystics as passionate women. In
the following chapter, we return to the theme of passion to
examine its roots, show how it is present in medieval mystical
texts, and suggest ways in which passionate love for God can
be an asset in living a spiritual life.

While readers may be moved by the intensity of feeling with which these mystics express themselves, we also notice the convincing integration of feeling within the complexity of the entire human person and a clear rejection of feeling as a "warm fuzzy" rather than as loving commitment to God and neighbor. There is no doubt about the intellectual genius of many of these women. Hildegard towers above most medieval figures in the breadth of her erudition; Julian of Norwich spends most of her adult life seeking understanding of her religious experience; and truth is the focus of Catherine of Siena's life and work. As we will see in chapter 4, one of the most poetic, insightful, and compelling descriptions of the relationship between love and reason is found in a letter Hadewijch of Brabant writes to a sister beguine. Hadewijch speaks of love and reason as the two eyes of charity. Both are crucial components of the journey and both are susceptible to overstepping their bounds.[68]

On other levels as well, readers find themselves jolted awake. It is impossible to enter into this world and remain indifferent. At the least, we have noted how one is brought up short by often startling language and imagery. The creative statement of paradox is a hallmark of mystical writing. Julian and Mechtild find God in the lowliest of bodily functions and Hadewijch's last of seven names for Love is hell.[69] Such works are abundant reservoirs of linguistic and metaphorical creativity. These women are teachers of awe and wonder and intense involvement with life. In spite of life–threatening illness and internal and external challenge, they retain their ability to be surprised, indeed to be amazed at, the love that God has for them and for all of creation. We sense that they can hardly believe the depths of both the pain and the joy of following Christ.

Many of these medieval women are what I call "one–trackers," that is, they give themselves wholeheartedly to the enterprise of life–giving love. Terms like *singleness of purpose* and *purity of heart* express this attitude of intense commitment and engagement. Catherine of Siena begins many of her prayers with repeated exclamations such as "O Godhead! Godhead! Eternal Godhead!"[70] or "Christ love! Christ love!"[71] Hadewijch of Brabant envisions herself as a knight whose shield has warded off so many stabs that there is no room for a single additional gash.[72] One is reminded of the psalmist who is deeply enmeshed in relationship with Yahweh: "Hear my voice, O God, in my complaint; preserve my life from the dread enemy. Hide me from the secret plots of the wicked, from the scheming of evildoers, who whet their tongues like swords, who aim bitter words like arrows, shooting from ambush at the blameless; they shoot suddenly and without fear" (Ps 64:1–4). In another vein, Hildegard expresses her deep feelings in spontaneous song: "But I also brought forth songs with their melody, in praise of God and the saints, without being taught by anyone, and I sang them too, even though I had never learnt either musical notation or any kind of singing."[73]

As we read these texts, many of us find that our own feelings begin slowly to come to life. These women challenge the dull, flat, lukewarm dimensions of existence, not by berating or condemning us, but simply by being their own spontaneous, real, committed selves. The life of their feelings is contagious. We cannot feast on a steady diet of their words and images and remain indifferent to the joy and pathos of existence. Gradually, our own ability to laugh, to weep, to dance and sing, to importune and to celebrate is rejuvenated. Hearts of stone turn to hearts of flesh and deadness is transformed into life.

Conclusion

For many persons, elements of the intense committed relationships these women describe offer an alternative or complement to other types of spirituality. In addition to their reliance on experience, their hopefulness, and expression of intense affections, they appeal to us because of their courage, their intelligence, and—with some cultural adjustments—the strong model of womanhood they offer. At the least they are intriguing. But for some, they offer a tantalizing and exciting spiritual path. And if we are susceptible to their confidence and hope, we leave the texts with a sense that God's statement to Julian reveals an important truth: "I may make all things well, and I can make all things well, and I shall make all things well, and I will make all things well; and you will see yourself that every kind of thing will be well."[74]

We turn now to a more detailed exploration of the meaning of passion and the role of intense feeling in mystical writing in chapter 2, and examine the presence of passion in the work of two very different medieval mystics—Hildegard of Bingen and Hadewijch of Brabant—in chapters 3 and 4. Mystical texts are deeply theological, but they express theological ideas in poetic rather than systematic form. One of the hallmarks of poetry is its capacity to embrace feeling and to convey and arouse deep emotion in its readers. The following examination of the role of passion in the texts of two medieval women mystics can sensitize us to the contours and the importance of emotion in these classic texts, and invite greater awareness of, and freedom to embrace, strong feelings in our spiritual lives. The call to awaken affective engagement is an ancient promise of the Judeo–Christian tradition: "A new heart I will give you; and a new spirit I will put within you; and I will remove from your body the heart of stone and give you a heart of flesh" (Ezek 36:26).

Chapter 2

Passion in the Christian Tradition

We have grown out of and impatient of the language of the heart. And so even where there is a true emotion, we easily falsify it, through sheer crudity of perception.

Simon Tugwell[1]

Background

Definition

What exactly does the term *passion* mean? Working toward a definition is difficult since the experience of passion is very personal, often elusive, and resists precise categorization. But it is possible to limn the substance and basic parameters of the term, even though it encompasses a wide variety of meanings.[2] To begin, we might see passion as a particularly intense form of love.[3] Perhaps poets best capture the spirit of love's height, depth, breadth, and width. William Blake writes, "And we are put on earth a little space/That we may learn to bear the beams of love (*Songs of Innocence and of Experience*)." For Christians, God's love is most visible in Jesus Christ, the model for generous, tender, honest, joyous, and self–sacrificing dispositions and activity. In some cultures, market forces create a pseudo–love through exploitative and pornographic associations linked to sexuality and the commercialization of the body. As a result, university students generally balk at the idea that passionate love might inform their spiritual selves, or that genuine sexual encounter might bear the divine within it.

The narrower term *passion* also suggests a range of meanings. It has to do with the suffering of pain, such as any painful disorder of the body, mind, or spirit. In Christian terms it refers to the Passion of Jesus or the suffering of the martyrs. Second, *passion*, as the word itself suggests, implies passivity, that is, being acted upon by external agency. The derivative, *compassion*, implies the ability to suffer with another, to empathize with another's distress and to desire and work for its alleviation. Third, and perhaps most commonly, *passion* is connected with sexual desires and impulses, with love, romance, and strong amorous feelings. Less often, we use the term *passion* to speak of proneness toward hot–tempered irascibility. The term can also be used more broadly to speak of an eager outreaching of the mind toward something, an overmastering zeal or enthusiasm for a particular object. We say, "She is passionate about her work."

This mosaic of meanings helps us explore the variety of ways in which passion can play a life–giving role in the spiritual life. Theology too can benefit from the presence of passion. If we define theology as ordered reflection on the Christian life—a life eminently characterized by relationship—then theology must attend carefully to human relationships marked by desires, enthusiasms, frustrations, and sufferings in the context of a total life story in which one is both actor and acted upon. The net is widely cast—self, others, the cosmos, and God.

Greek Roots

Over two thousand years ago, Aristotle coined a word, *pathe*, to refer to a wide range of feelings, from anger and fear to joy and affection.[4] Today, we use the term *emotion* to cover the same ground, including the term *passion*, seen as an intense or even violent form of emotion. In the West, the meaning of passion has been significantly influenced by Greek thought. Love, characterized by *eros*, and nonmutuality, involved an intense longing to possess a valued object. Reciprocal (but not necessarily sexual) love was called *philia*, and involved mutual benefit to both parties. *Agape* was the term used for love that was nonsexual, selfless, and benevolent. The idea of passion was also linked to the divine. For the Greeks, the sense of divine presence was universal—no aspect of life was excluded a priori from association with the divine. There were sacred places set aside for various cults, but in general, the primary locus of the divine was the entire cosmos. We find the second–century Neoplatonist,

Plotinus, writing, "All the place is holy, and there is nothing which is without a share of soul."[5] E. H. Armstrong comments, "When the perceived environment of worship was the whole town or the whole countryside, it was hardly possible for the worshippers to feel that they were a special flock, a people set apart, separate from the whole world of nature and the common society of humanity."[6]

In the Greek pantheon, passionate, sexual love was associated with Aphrodite, the goddess of love, and her son, Eros. In ancient thought, one version of the creation story held that the world came about as the result of the coupling of divine powers and sexual generation, an event that endowed such coupling with distinctive importance.[7] Aphrodite and Eros embodied sexual charm, and the excitement that sometimes led to divine madness. Their power too was universal and included the wilder and more disorderly passions as well as those of traditional mating and married love.[8] The full expression of love—madness was not a daily occurrence, and Aphrodite and Eros were also felt to be present in a wide variety of ordinary expressions of sexual love. In the ancient Mediterranean world, "the wild as well as the tame, that which breaks all bounds and destroys all order as well as that which maintains order, had its place in the divine nature of things."[9]

Plato's famous story of the chariot's winged horses (the passions) being guided and controlled by the charioteer (reason) provides insight into his view of the passions. In the upper world, mighty Zeus holds the reins of the winged chariot, leading the way, ordering all and taking care of all. But in the lower world, weak souls plunge and tread on one another in confusion.[10] But in general, Greek thought regarded the passions as dangerous, less—than—human forces that were to be controlled, circumscribed, and subordinated to reason. The godlike quality of reason was the supreme value, and all of life was to be brought under its sway.

For Aristotle as well, true love was governed by reasoned choice, not by feeling or passion. But Aristotle takes Plato's emphasis on reason a step further. While Plato placed the desiring love of *eros* at the heart of all love, Aristotle used the term *philia* to describe genuine friendship and relegated *eros* to sexual love, a love that he saw as inferior to the love of friendship. Aristotle distinguishes three types of love.[11] The first is the love of utility, in which one person loves another for personal benefit. Using another person for one's own gain was looked upon as abuse, rather than as a legitimate form of relationship. Second is the love of pleasure, in which persons love each other because it is enjoyable. Both benefit from the fruits of the relationship. The third type of love is a selfless love, the only true friendship, in which one loves others because of who they are in themselves. A true friend is one who cares about the welfare of the other person and wishes her well. Reason has an especially important role in this highest form of love.

Later philosophical forms of Greek piety took on a more austerely ethical nature that severely curtailed expressions of *eros*. It was only at the highest level of human thought that *eros* could be safely admitted. Stoic philosophers in the fourth century BCE included the love of wisdom, as well as feeling and emotion in their concept of reason. They distinguished between good desires and feelings that were part of reason, and passions and mental perturbations that were present in a soul whose reasoning faculty was disordered.[12]

Jewish and Christian Appropriation

Christian writers, influenced by Greek thought, converted its rich philosophical and contemplative traditions to Christian ends.[13] In the process, they also absorbed Greek skepticism about the value of the emotions. H. Howard Bloch traces this history that pits reason, form, activity, and maleness against emotion, body, passivity, and femaleness. He discusses Philo (c.

20 BCE – c. 50 CE), a key Jewish philosopher known for his synthesis of Judaism and Middle Platonism, as an example of an author who subordinated passion to reason. For example, in his analysis of the creation story in Genesis, Philo layered a Hellenistic interpretation on a Jewish story in order to establish the superiority of mind over body. In this view, Eve is seen as helper (associated with passion), one who is both created from, and thus subsequent to, Adam (associated with mind). For Philo, the deeper meaning of this story is that "sense and the passions are helpers of the soul and come after the soul."[14]

The Greek word for "passionlessness" is *apatheia*, a concept appropriated for Christianity by Clement of Alexandria and the monks who fled to the desert in the fourth century.[15] Evagrius Ponticus associates *apatheia* with the glory and light of the soul, a state of tranquility and detachment, a precondition for pure prayer, and the source of *agape*.[16] In an environment in which passions had a negative connotation, they gradually became associated with vice, eclipsing any potential for virtue. But a more common understanding saw passion, not as evil, but as a force that needed to be tamed and ordered. To seek *apatheia* meant to seek freedom from enslaving cravings and addictions in order to develop peace and harmony in the soul.[17] But Gregory of Nyssa offered an alternate view. He held that while unrestrained desire in human passion was wrong, "passion for bodiless things is passionless"—and so in the spiritual realm, we should love as strongly and madly as possible.[18] In his homilies on the Song of Songs, Gregory of Nyssa writes, "The soul must transform passion into passionlessness so that when every corporeal affection has been quenched, our mind may seethe with passion for the spirit alone...."[19] The vehicle for spiritual passion was the spiritual senses.

In the Middle Ages, Bernard of Clairvaux writes eloquently about the ordering of the affections. Even though Bernard treats the flesh in more positive terms than many mystical writers, he consistently subordinates carnal to spiritual love. In his hierarchy of loves, carnal love of Christ is needed in order to drive out the lower false sweetness of illicit human love. His metaphor is bracing—"Sweetness conquers sweetness as one nail drives out another."[20] In turn, one must abandon the carnal love of Christ in favor of a higher spiritual way of loving.

In writing about the spiritual life, early Christian writers both relied on, and transformed, these Hellenistic ideas about the passions. The basic trajectory of the spiritual journey was to move "up," away from matter and emotion and toward a more spiritual, abstract realm, devoid of reference to the physical senses. In the third century, Origen initiated a tradition called the "spiritual senses" in which he transposed the five physical senses onto a spiritual plane. Thus, authors spoke of seeing, touching, tasting, smelling, and hearing God in a way that was analogous, but superior, to ordinary daily sense perceptions.[21] Origen writes, "[J]ust as there is said to be a fleshly love, which the poets also call Love, according to which the person who loves sows in the flesh, so also there is a spiritual love according to which the inner man, when he loves, sows in the Spirit (Gal 6:8)."[22]

However, with the incarnation at the center of Christian theology and spirituality, it would have been impossible for Christians to follow the lead of those Greek thinkers and practitioners who viewed the body, sexuality, and the passions as evil. Various types of dualistic worldviews emerged regularly throughout history—Zoroastrianism, Manichaeism, Gnosticism, Docetism, Catharism, Albigensianism. But Christianity consistently resisted these strains. Since they believe that God created the world and sent his Son into it as a human being, Christians view creation as a gift of God that is both good and beautiful. Thus, the tradition reflects a tension between Christian dogma and the Hellenistic milieu in which Christianity grew. Christians saw creation as the starting point of the spiritual life. But Greek influence shows up in descriptions of the later stages of the journey in which Christians were to leave behind meditation on material creation and Christ's humanity in order to enter the higher spiritual and immaterial reaches of the spiritual life.

Patristic authors like Origen (d. c. 253), Gregory of Nyssa (d. 394), Evagrius of Ponticus (d. 399), and John Cassian (d. c. 435) provided the foundation for later Christian mystical theology.[23] Their legacy is a creative synthesis of Greek thought transformed by their Christian faith, their experience of the desert, and their creative dedication to purity of heart. They emphasized the need to purify desire in order to unite with God—in response to God's intense desire to reach out to humanity. In the Prologue to his *Commentary on the Song of Songs*, Origen emphasizes that the Song is only for the spiritually mature: "[J]ust as children are not moved to the passion of love, so neither is the age of the inner man, if it is that of a little one and an infant, allowed to grasp these words."[24] But the mature person is led by a heavenly love and desire that is drawn to the beauty of the Word of God. She falls in love with God's splendor and receives a "dart and wound of love" that burns "with the blessed fire" of God's love.[25] Origen even goes so far as to say, "I do not think one could be blamed if one called God Passionate Love (*eros/amor*), just as God called him Charity (*agape/caritas*)... you must take whatever scripture says about charity (*caritas*) as if it had been said in reference to passionate love (*amor*), taking no notice of the difference in terms; for the same meaning is conveyed by both."[26]

When we read texts of early and medieval Christian spiritual writers who devalue or even condemn the passions, we need to keep three things in mind. First, these writers did not relegate emotion and reason to separate, tightly sealed compartments. Rather, they viewed the human person in an integral way—thought was not necessarily devoid of feeling, nor did feeling

43

lack cognitive content. Feelings and thought were aspects or perspectives of a single human person. Nevertheless, and this is the second point, emotions *were* suspect and seen as inferior to rational activity. Third, when mystical writers refer to the passions in a negative way, they usually have in mind passions that are *disordered*, oriented to sinful movements of the soul such as lust and selfishness.[27] Thus, when Gregory of Nyssa counsels ascetic practices such as fasting and celibacy, his primary aim is not the repression of sexual passion but the purification and education of base desires, so that they can be reoriented toward God and the Good.[28]

The privileging of the spiritual and intellectual over the carnal has had a long run in the Christian tradition, even to the present. Like the Greeks before them, theologians often discuss love in terms of a threefold hierarchy. *Eros* is at the bottom and points to acquisitive, sensual, passionate, and sexual expressions of love. It is selfish and grasping, and almost always carries a negative connotation. *Philia* comes next—a dutiful love, such as that between parents and children, or friends. At the top is *agape* or charity, the noblest form of love that reflects God's love. It is altruistic, compassionate, and self–sacrificing. This schema keeps alive a lingering skepticism about the goodness of the passions and sexual expression. The inferior status assigned to the body and "erotic" passions has been particularly onerous for women, with whom these qualities are culturally associated. Indeed it is with a deep sense of both justice and irony that we turn to medieval women to recover these important aspects of human life.

Neglect and Devaluation of Affectivity

Questions about the meaning of love have occupied philosophers, musicians, poets, theologians, and ordinary people since the dawn of civilization.[29] As we have seen, the way humans speak about love and its relationship to reason changes from age to age. The Renaissance, Enlightenment, and Modernity each had its particular version, with many variations within each period. In the Christian church, theology continues to be associated with reason, and mysticism with the affections. Before the fourteenth century, this distinction would have been unheard of. Even someone as cerebral as Thomas Aquinas saw the meaning and goal of theology as love of God. In the late medieval period, there was a divorce between theology and what today we call spirituality. In addition to changes in theological specialization and methodology, the divorce was eventually extended to embrace a deep separation between the affective dimension of religious experience linked with "piety", and the more rationalistic, conceptual forms of theological analysis. But fissures are emerging in this long trajectory of devaluing emotion. In the recent past, there has been a growing awareness of the need to recover this aspect of human existence and a new hunger for the emotional dimensions of living.[30]

In the United States, the '60s phenomenon was one visible manifestation of this hunger breaking forth. Initially, many Christians turned to traditions—mostly Eastern—that continued to value the affections, and that did not privilege reason and thought at the expense of feeling. Many Americans found their way to ashrams in India to study with gurus and recover a more holistic spirituality. Since then, some have found a permanent home in various forms of Eastern religions, but many have returned to their Christian roots to explore more deeply forgotten or neglected resources that might awaken, form, and renew the affective and mystical dimensions of the spiritual life. Regrettably, the Christian mystical tradition is still one of the best–kept secrets among Christian believers.

Until the very recent past, exploration of the theoretical aspects of love has been singularly neglected by psychoanalysts, biological and social scientists, historians, humanists, and espe-

cially theologians.[31] Even the topic of friendship was infrequently addressed by scholars in the twentieth century.[32]
"Passion" is absent from many subject catalogues in libraries, is
rarely chosen as a title for books or articles, and is invisible in
indices where one would expect to find the term. The researcher
is forced to comb texts from a variety of disciplines, hoping to
find a chapter here, or a single paragraph there, dealing with
passion.[33] When the topic of passion does come up, it appears in
discussions on affectivity, sexuality, sin, or crime—and almost
never in analyses of religious experience. The topic of romantic
love often suffers the same fate. The Columbia Psychoanalytic
Center in New York reported that it had no trouble funding
symposia on individualism, narcissism, and the limits of truth,
but ran into difficulty when the topic was romantic love.[34]

Freud

Blame for devaluing the emotions is often laid at the feet of
Sigmund Freud. In particular, critics point to Freud's thesis that
narcissism drives all forms of love, reducing love to the desire to
be loved. This viewpoint strikes at the heart of altruistic love and
surely at the Christian idea of selfless love of God, neighbor,
and even enemy. Is this ideal for which the mystics prayed, and
by which they lived, but an illusion or even a delusion—a cir-
cuitous device to satisfy love of self?[35] Happily, on this point,
Freud has not had the last word. The dialogue his work engen-
dered has both supplemented and corrected his ideas about
love.[36] But Freud's understanding of love as narrowly self–interested does not exhaust his legacy regarding the affections.
Indeed, a goal of psychoanalysis is to help people remove obstacles that prevent them from loving well, freeing them to love
(and work) in healthier, more productive and fulfilling ways. In
this sense, Freud's thought has been a major catalyst in prodding
Western culture to attend to the affections, to value them, and

to take them seriously by sorting out constructive and destructive ways of loving.[37]

Literature

In a culture in which intellectual reflection on forms of love
is rare, poets and novelists must carry more than their share of
the weight, becoming the champions and standard–bearers of
love.[38] But in the view of novelist and commentator Roxana
Robinson, even in the world of literature, there are signs of a
cooling down. In an article entitled "The Big Chill," Robinson
contrasts the heart–filled literature of a century ago (for example, *Pere Goriot, Anna Karenina*) with contemporary literature that
she describes as emotionally barren. When we read these earlier
novels, "emotion seized us, took us over, broke us down."[39]
Robinson also recalls the moving stories of Oedipus, Achilles,
Lear, Othello, Jane Eyre, and David Copperfield. How do we
react when we read that Achilles, "that most macho of men,"
wept for three days after the death of Patroclus? Or what can we
learn from Augustine's account of the death of his best friend
Alypius in *The Confessions?* Today, she says, such deep affective
engagement is rare. "Passion is largely absent from our books: an
icy chill has crept across the writer's landscape."[40]

Robinson also blames literary criticism for its contribution
to the retreat from passion. Not unlike formal theology, literary
criticism aspired increasingly to imitate the rubrics of the exact
sciences. Its language became "dry, esoteric and professional,"
stripping away the subjective language of feeling that does not
easily lend itself to scientific observation.[41] With critical focus
on the value of the intellect, writes Robinson, we have lost the
"whole turbulent landscape of feeling."[42]

Clearly, one must protest such a wholesale generalization.[43]
What is emotionally barren for one reader will be emotionally
engaging for another. And surely we can be grateful that world
literature still touches readers' affections, moving us to positive

feelings of love and compassion. But Robinson's lament motivates me to reflect on trends that have led to the devaluation or marginalization of the affections. Preference for alienation, chilling irony, disaffection, and distance eclipses passion, tenderness, engagement, anguish, and rapture—in art, music, literature, film, and even daily conversation.[44] To what extent are these tendencies present and to what extent do they influence us, perhaps unconsciously?

Cultural Factors

Happily, there are beginning signs of a turnaround in the theoretical interest in the emotions. In a recent article entitled "Getting Emotional," Scott McLemee traces recent developments in the academic study of emotion.[45] He distinguishes between the presence of emotion in the primary documents of history and literature—"emotion has always been at the core of the humanities"—and formal scholarly reflection on emotion itself. The literature he reviews is from sociology, political science, literary criticism, psychology, and neurophysiology. Studies on particular emotions focus on anger[46] and shame,[47] while other authors voice concern about the commercialization of feeling.[48] Virtually absent from the list are scholarly works in the fields of ethics, theology, or spirituality.

The Greek legacy that genders emotion, linking it with women, remains alive and well. Society gives women permission to express emotion and then criticizes them for it. In general, this worldview associates emotion with weakness and sentimentality, traits that are devalued and even ridiculed. Tears seem naïve and childish, causing embarrassment and shame. They signal lack of control. In teaching mystical texts, I find it more and more challenging to explain to students the meaning of the "gift of tears"—once a precious spiritual gift described by saints and theologians. The American portrait of the tough, cool "cowboy" provides a contrasting image. The cowboy is a loner, with tough skin and an unexpressive heart.[49]

A further consideration is the thorny problem of the effect of sustained exposure to gratuitous violence in games, movies and television, and to daily exposure on the evening news to the enormities of human suffering across the globe. The media deliver more horror—real and fictionalized—than we can cope with, and out of self–protection, we may opt to shut down emotionally and disengage from affective involvement with the world. In complex ways, exposure to violence can both numb and evoke affective responses. The experience of the terrorist attack on New York City and Washington DC on September 11, 2001, brought forth a flood of kindness and compassion, but living in an environment of sustained violence, whether in real life, in the media, or in games, can clearly cause a dulling of one's emotional responses. Finally, one can point to the study of emotion from chemical and psychobiological perspectives. Scientists are in the process of linking specific emotions with chemical levels and brain functions—developments whose import is yet to be calculated.[50]

In the midst of all this complexity, it remains important that we produce art, music, literature, philosophy, theology, and spirituality that elicit altruistic feelings that lead to commitment, compassion, and action for the good of the world. We must seek continually to name and nurture the forces that help us to know and form our affections in creative and productive ways. There are some hopeful signs in new conversations about the role of the affections. Important contributors include Bernard McGinn and E. Ann Matter in historical theology;[51] Martha Nussbaum, Rita Nakashima Brock, and William Spohn in ethics;[52] Don Saliers on prayer and the affections;[53] and new translations and interpretations of the Song of Songs.[54] We turn now to the specific issue of the relationship between the affections and reason.

The Affections and Reason:
Rivals or Partners?

Knowledge and Love

The mystical tradition is a valuable locus for exploration of the range and complexity of the relationship between *amor* and *intellectus*. Bernard McGinn traces the intricate patterns of the relationship of knowledge and love in the medieval mystical tradition and cautions against simplistic oppositions. The popular medieval phrase—"love itself is a kind of knowing (*amor ipse intellectus est)*"—captures the belief that human desire remains linked to the intelligible even when it goes beyond reason itself. This type of knowing was not divorced from love but susceptible to it—becoming wisdom under its sway. In the form of wisdom, love included knowledge, and knowledge was infused with love. The medieval distinction between reason (*ratio*) and knowing (*intellectus* or *intelligentia*) suggests the existence of such a "higher, intuitive awareness beyond conceptual knowing."[55]

This harmonious integration of knowledge and love gradually became obscured. By the fourteenth century, the author of the *Cloud of Unknowing*, privileging love, would reject reason as incapable of reaching union with God. Several hundred years later, influenced by what some see as a superficial reading of philosophers from Descartes to Kant and Nietzsche, Western sensibilities gradually embraced separation over relationship, and a narrowly defined reason became the privileged *lingua franca* in the West.[56] The late twentieth century began to correct this dualist epistemology. Among others, feminist writers argue for the important ways in which all kinds of emotions contribute to knowing. In turn, knowledge contributes to the formation of appropriate emotions. Allison Jaggar writes that reflection on emotions is central to systematic knowledge. All human faculties are interdependent, each representing an aspect of human knowing inseparable from the others.[57]

Part of the fallout from the separation of feeling and thought was a devaluing of the humanities in the academy, including religious studies. A condition of acceptance in the broader intellectual community required that religious studies appropriate narrowly empirical, rationalistic criteria for truth. This development has resulted not only in the exclusion of religion from curricula, but has created a rift between mysticism and theology. One of the most obvious differences between mystical and formal theological expression is style. Formal systematic theology takes its cue from philosophy, attends to logic and order, seeks to eliminate contradictions and unclear statements, and often employs a very specialized technical vocabulary. It values distance and scholarly objectivity. Mystical literature, on the other hand, resembles poetry. The language is fluid and suggestive. It evokes feelings and aims primarily to move the reader to holiness of life rather than to communicate ideas. It relies on paradox, metaphor, image, and symbol to convey the "more" of the human experience of the divine. Instead of being cool and removed, its expression is marked by engagement and passionate energy.[58]

Vernacular Theology

Bernard McGinn characterizes medieval theology as a conversation among three different types of theology: the monastic voice, developed in the eleventh and twelfth centuries and represented by someone like Bernard of Clairvaux; the scholastic voice, shaped at the newly founded universities and visible in the *Summa theologiae* of Thomas Aquinas; and vernacular theology, a much more diffuse and diverse form of discourse found in lives of the saints and accounts of visions. Vernacular theology employed diverse linguistic strategies to express new and creative innovations. Poetry was one such strategy. Although the use of poetry to express mystical consciousness was not unknown in the earlier tradition, it "grew in significance in vernacular theology."[59] While it is advantageous to distinguish among these different settings and styles of medieval theology, it does not follow that one or the other form was characterized by reason to the exclusion of feeling, or vice versa.

In vernacular theology, the impassioned nature of many descriptions of the soul's ascent to God has been judged as mentally unbalanced and hysterical on the one hand, or, more recently, as an important breakthrough beyond the more "restrained intellectualized conceptions" of scholastic theology.[60] These contrasting judgments raise issues about the relationship between reason and emotion in mystical experience and theology. Contemporary anthropological understandings seek to account for the fullness of human life, emphasizing connections and unity rather than separation. As a result, the lines between reason and emotion have softened, since we no longer view the capacities of the human person in tight, compartmentalized spheres.

But even in this new environment in which the human person is viewed as a psychosomatic unity, it is helpful to continue to distinguish between reason, emotion, and imagination when we speak of human functioning.[61] For example, the concept of the affective can be useful to single out feeling states, moods, or emotions, such as anger, jealousy, or love, including their more passionate expressions. And the concept of reason legitimately points to elements such as explanation, evaluation, coherence, and logical argument. But the distinctions are made ultimately to be at the service of unity, not further polarization (*distinguer pour unir*). Emotion and reason are not enemies or polar opposites—with the presence of one necessarily driving out or devaluing the other. To distinguish between them does not suggest that feelings have no cognitive dimension, nor that cognition is devoid of feeling.

Contemporary Theology and Spirituality

Recent developments in psychology, in our understanding of sexuality, and even in the hard sciences—which are regularly discovering new connections and interdependencies among body–mind–spirit—have paved the way for a more rounded approach to the human person. These developments are salutary for theological and spiritual disciplines, which continue to wrestle with the historical trajectory of dualism in which emotion was judged to be inimical to the spiritual life.[62] But, as we have seen, in the broader two–thousand–year history of Christianity, the relationship between reason and love has been configured in a wide variety of ways.

At first blush, theology would seem by its very nature to exclude intense affections. For we think of theology primarily as a rational activity, and indeed it is. But if we are to take seriously the turn to the subject and the kind of holistic anthropology noted above, it is incumbent upon us to grapple with the ways in which theology is—indeed must be—an affective as well as an intellectual exercise. Canadian Jesuit theologian Bernard Lonergan (1904–85) included the affections in his treatment of theological method. He labels the fifth of eight methodological steps, "foundations," a category that refers to the conversion of the theologian. For some theologians, this conversion—what Lonergan calls "other–worldly falling in love"—is the first step in the theological task. Love of God then grounds both the way one does theology and the outcome of one's efforts, since the theologian who experiences intense love and commitment to God is different from one whose spiritual life is characterized by indifference or one who studies the tradition from an agnostic or atheistic perspective.[63]

The example of the saints is another way in which spirituality and theology can be influenced by the affections. From the origins of Christianity to the present, the historical record shows how affective energy can be brought to life by the example of those who are deeply in love with God. The primordial model for Christians, of course, is Jesus Christ, the theological center of the Christian tradition. Throughout this tradition, there are numerous cases of conversions mediated by reading lives of the saints. Francis of Assisi and Ignatius of Loyola are well–known examples. Closer to home, we can point to "saints" among family, friends, or co–workers who inspired us to love God with more fire than we thought possible. Even if theology has not traditionally turned to narrative forms of expression, it is important that it stay connected to the spiritual energy and passion that breathes forth from the stories of the holy ones. Indeed, Michael Buckley suggests that the witness of the mystics provides a valuable element in contemporary arguments for the existence of God.[64]

Thus, accounts of mystical experience are important resources for information and understanding about how to talk about God more formally, and for what it means to be passionately in love with God and the world. In chapters 3 and 4, I uncover this evidence in some detail in the work of two medieval women mystics. But I also ask a further question about whether and how these mystical texts might infuse contemporary spirituality with new life, and theological thinking with greater insight. Can the expression of such mystical experience bring fresh perspectives that allow room for the affections to influence our thinking, our spiritualities, and our work as theologians? It is my contention that mystical texts can positively influence doctrine and theology as well as the spiritual life. This conviction requires acknowledging that mystical texts contain important theological material on a wide range of topics from the doctrine of God to grace, virtue, and eschatology.

Passion in Religious Experience

In spite of recent interest in the affections, wariness about physical love and passion perdures. We have noted how the more carefully calibrated medieval appreciation of the role of the affections and their relationship to knowledge became muted in the modern period when the passions were upstaged by the mind, and physical, sexual passion was constrained within narrow moral borders. Since passion is a staple of the human condition, such a negative attitude inevitably produces tension between human passion and the demands of the Christian life as they have been laid down in the tradition. Even today, with enormous emphasis placed on developing a holistic spirituality, the passions and sexuality are too often left out of the equation.

Although mystical experience remained an arena in which spiritual passion could be legitimately expressed, the link between human passion and religious experience grew more tenuous. Indeed, over the centuries, fear and mistrust of the passions grew to an extent that, in retrospect, seems paranoid. While it is difficult to distinguish clearly the various reasons for past cautious attitudes toward the power of the passions, it is imperative that we weigh critically the values of the past in the interest of the fullness of life in the present. More than two millennia after Plato, we remain bound and conflicted by these tensions. The task of increasing our understanding of the passions and returning them to their rightful place in our lives is yet to be satisfactorily addressed.

Religious Passion: Descriptions and Definitions

In our exploration of medieval women mystics' reflection on their encounters with God, I define *passion* as an intense form of affectivity, especially of love and desire between God and the human person. In addition to the adjective *intense*, we might also

55

employ terms like *strong, vehement, enthusiastic, ardent, zealous*. In other words, *passion* signifies an extreme form of both divine and human affectivity. I also want to describe passion as a mysterious impulse toward human wholeness and freedom. Passionate experience has the potential to open one's personality to grace, to lead one toward fuller self–knowledge, and to contribute to the ongoing creation of a new self as image of God.[65]

Passion functions to organize many aspects of an individual's life. It is that part of us that eschews mediocrity and facile compromise.[66] It creates a consuming longing in the lover that includes and extends beyond the beloved. While affect can be warm, passion is hot. It is often accompanied with sighs, tears, groaning. It makes one vulnerable to the pain that inevitably accompanies great love, and often finds its apogee in ecstasy, that momentary experience of being taken out of oneself to be united with the beloved, finding oneself in harmony with the totality of reality.[67]

Human and Divine Passion

We have seen that for Plato, the highest form of love is eminently rational, free from disturbing influences of passion. The object of this pure love is an impersonal ideal—Goodness itself. Love among humans has no place in this ethereal, idealized love. The primary difference in Christian love is that the ultimate object is no longer an impersonal ideal, but a personal God who is the fullness of love—in fact, Love itself.[68] Christianity teaches that love of God is the primary love. Other persons and things are to be loved because they reflect and lead to God. Without proper nuance, this way of talking about love can give the impression that human loves are secondary and peripheral rather than central to love of God. Intense love of God is seen as a spiritualized, mystical love, stripped of bodily, material, human, sexual connections. But it is precisely the experience of sexual love that gave rise to the language and metaphors of love used by the mystics in virtually every major religion. Lovers of God turned spontaneously to the experience of human passion to describe their encounters with God.

This use of the language and imagery of passion strikes many contemporary readers as strange—given the authors' celibate state—but it becomes dangerous when coupled with devaluation of bodiliness and the passions of physical love. An important theological and spiritual task is to discover fresh ways to link ordinary human love in all its forms with spiritual love. Healing this rift becomes even more imperative in a world in which we confront daily explicit images of sexual exploitation.

And to complicate matters further, we need to inquire not only about the obvious presence of human passion in mystical texts, but also the mystics' penchant to describe God in similar terms. Contemporary theologians also express this idea. Catherine LaCugna writes, "Because of God's outreach to the creature, God is said to be essentially relational, ecstatic, fecund, alive as passionate love."[69] What does it mean to have a passionate God?

The question of the presence of emotion in God has become a leitmotif of much recent theological work. But years before this discussion became prominent, Rosemary Haughton addressed the issue of passion in God. Her books, *The Passionate God* and *On Trying to Be Human*, reveal her attempt to take human passion seriously and to explore its connections to the gospel message.[70] In general, Haughton defines passion as the drive of powerful emotion toward the knowledge and, in some sense, the possession of an object outside oneself.[71]

For Haughton, the experience of passion can bring a sense of liberation from ordinary life, a profound increase in genuine self–knowledge, with its concomitant maturity, a renewed pattern of activity that perdures after the "feeling" of passion subsides, and a broadening of one's understanding of life beyond law and custom. All of this takes place in the context of relationship. The gospel calls us to be free to fall in love with other persons, and Haughton regards the sexual expression of passion as the prototype of all passion because by its nature it contains within itself the conditions for its own development toward wholeness.[72]

In *The Passionate God*, Haughton explores the radical implications of the poetic and scandalous statement that God became, and remains, human.[73] Only a love of intense passion on God's part can account for this gift to the world. With the incarnation and resurrection of Jesus as fulcra, Haughton builds a theology with the help of the language and concepts of the romantic–love tradition. For Haughton, central to this tradition are the ideas of "breakthrough" and "exchange." The paradigm of "breakthrough" is the incarnation in which the divine breaks into the sphere of the human. This breakthrough has several consequences. One of the most important is that it makes nonsense of the usual commonsense ways in which we divide reality into the material and the spiritual. Second, incarnation affects not only human beings but "involves every level of reality from the most basic particles to the ultimate Being of God."[74] The incarnation makes holy all materiality, including bodiliness.

Haughton further suggests that the medieval category of "being" rings in the modern ear as a static concept. It has what she calls a "stopped" quality. Therefore she prefers to speak about the totality of life in terms of love rather than in terms of being, since love implies dynamic relationship.[75] Love cannot be love unless it is given and received, that is, "exchanged."[76] This exchange goes on everywhere, from the intimate recesses of the Trinity to the lowliest form of matter.[77] For Haughton, the language of romantic passion provides the "concepts, images and language tools that enable us to articulate the theology of exchange."[78] The images of passion, she says, are images of love in action, pointing to some kind of breakthrough to an encounter that is perceived as difficult.[79]

It is easy to imagine Jesus walking the earth in his gentle, determined, healing way. It is also easy for most of us to imagine deity as the infinitely loving creator of the universe. It may not even be hard for us to imagine the Persons of the Trinity engaged in intimate mutual exchange. But a totally unimaginable oneness, a divine passion so intense that God *has* to be Jesus and a Jesus so passionate he *has* to be God—this is so "outrageous a demand on the human intellect and human courage that there are only two possible responses: utter faith or utter rejection."[80]

Haughton extends the metaphor of a passionate God when she describes the passion God has for human persons. This divine love works for, in, through, and among people, embracing the "entire, mysterious and infinitely complex system of interrelationships which is creation."[81] In particular, she believes that we gain insight into the passion that drove God to become incarnate by looking carefully at the way people love each other, especially in passionate ways, "because that kind of love tells us things about how love operates which we could not otherwise know."[82]

But in spite of this creative theological analysis of passion, questions about the role of passion remain. Is it possible for us to benefit in concrete, practical ways from learning about the passionate love of the mystics? Is it realistic, or even desirable, to rehabilitate sexual passion in a Christian context, to envision a harmony between intense sexual experience and the rest of one's life—in particular one's life as a disciple of Christ?[83] Does our heightened awareness of the dangers of passionate love banish it from discourse about our relationship with God?

Some persons may react negatively to the recovery of the passionate dimensions of life, fearing loss of reason and chaos. This may be due to the penchant in the Christian tradition to pay inordinate attention to sinful expressions of passionate love. We have always seemed more concerned about sins of the flesh than sins of the mind. However, this pattern of emphasis on the negative aspects of passion, with a concomitant preference for order and rationality, has had deeply troubling consequences in the lack of attention to healthy passions and how to nurture them. Proper attention to the affections includes not only appreciation, but also formation and discipline. There is a need to guard against sentimentality, egoistic love, and love that is grounded in illusion, as well as a call to help believers to develop free, intense, and selfless patterns of love.

In an essay entitled "The Nature of Passionate Love," Milton Viederman lists as enemies of passion: total understanding of the other, familiarity, certainty, predictability, absolute trust in the other, the disarming of jealousy, and legitimization of the relationship.[84] This list opens a vista onto the geography of passion that can be applied to one's relationship with God. For example, some mystics give voice to a sense of God's jealousy. It is also the case that total understanding of God is no more possible than total understanding of another person. The mystical literature is filled with the sense that God is constantly surprising those God loves. It can also be the case that inappropriate trust in, and familiarity with, God arise from arrogance and lead to taking God for granted.

Thus, the task before us is to explore the horizons of our understanding of passion and to read the medieval mystical tradition in order to discover ways in which the presence of passion can enhance existence—in body, in thought, and in the spiritual journey. We take for granted that passion drives great poets, thieves, scientists, warriors, and lovers. But surely passion cannot be the exclusive domain of the famous and infamous. While one could argue that certain individuals possess personality structures that lend themselves to lives of intense passion, it is more important to note that passion can be present anywhere, and assume the coloring of any personality. This broader conception of passion opens up the possibility that everyone has the potential to nurture passion in marriage, learning, appreciating nature, child rearing, attitudes toward injustice, and the spiritual life. Is it not the case that, in some sense, a life devoid of passion, like a life devoid of reflection, is a life not worth living?

Images of Love in the Tradition

We have described tradition as a past that is necessarily and intimately linked to the present and the future. Since tradition is not something "out there" upon which to gaze and about which to make judgments, our exploration of the role of passion in medieval spiritual life is directly linked to present concerns. What happened *then* is part of a process that continues *now*, and that will, in turn, lead us into the future. On the one hand, we mediate the tradition by making intelligent decisions about it. On the other hand, the tradition mediates us, that is, our understanding of the tradition forms the basis of our own development. We are always in the stream of this process.[85]

The evidence of passionate engagement in descriptions of religious experience has been a constant throughout the Judeo–Christian tradition. The prophets express passion for justice (Isa 56; Jer 21); the psalms overflow with passionate feeling; and Paul's letters reveal the intensity with which he preached the good news (1 Cor 15).

The beautiful poetry of the Psalms, Israel's prayer book, is replete with expressions of a wide range of emotion.

> O God, you are my God, I seek you,
>   my soul thirsts for you;
> my flesh faints for you,
>   as in a dry and weary land where there is no water.
> So I have looked upon you in the sanctuary
>   beholding your power and glory.

Because your steadfast love is better than life,
   my lips will praise you.
So I will bless you as long as I live;
   I will lift up my hands and call on your name.

My soul is satisfied as with a rich feast,
   and my mouth praises you with joyful lips
when I think of you on my bed,
   and meditate on you in the watches of the night;
for you have been my help,
   and in the shadow of your wings I sing for joy.
My soul clings to you; your right hand upholds me.
   (Ps 63:1–8)

Throughout the tradition, biblical images of love in its many forms have been the inspiration and model for countless mystics who sought to capture in language their experiences of God. While all describe these experiences as ineffable, they nevertheless struggle to communicate what the experience was like in order to inspire and instruct the reader in the mystical way.

Wisdom

Those books of the Hebrew biblical canon known as "wisdom literature" have played a prominent role in accounts of mystical experience.[86] While the prophets addressed social responsibility through attention to the legal demands of the covenant, the wisdom writers were more interested in the broader questions of life and human experience, including the affections. Wisdom seeks to integrate the ideals of faith into the practical experience of everyday life.[87] In the midst of his suffering, Job asks, "Where then does wisdom come from? And where is the place of understanding?" (Job 28:20).

Often personified as a woman, "Wisdom cries out in the street; in the squares she raises her voice....I will pour out my thoughts to you; I will make my words known to you" (Prov 1:20, 23). Wisdom was present at the creation of the world: "The Lord created me [Wisdom] at the beginning of his work, the first of his acts of long ago. Ages ago I was set up, at the first, before the beginning of the earth" (Prov 8:22–23).

Jewish and Christian feminist theologians have turned to the Hebrew wisdom tradition in order to recover female dimensions of God. The Greek word for wisdom is *Sophia* (*hokmah* in Hebrew; *sapientia* in Latin). Elizabeth Johnson describes Wisdom–Sophia as "the most developed personification of God's presence and activity in the Hebrew Scriptures, much more acutely limned than Spirit, torah, or word."[88] Pointing to God's gracious goodness in creating the world, Sophia is leader, "preacher in Israel, the taskmaster, and creator God. She seeks people, finds them on the road, invites them to dinner. She offers life, rest, knowledge, and salvation to those who accept her.... She is a people–loving spirit who shares the throne of God."[89]

Scholars point out that Sophia was a term early Christians associated with Jesus. Elisabeth Schüssler Fiorenza notes that the earliest Palestinian theological memory and interpretation of Jesus' life and death saw him as Sophia's messenger, and later, as Sophia herself.[90] Like Sophia, Jesus is associated with creative power, order, law, justice, and understanding (John 1:1–18). Sophia represents passionate engagement, solidarity with those who suffer, and renewing energy. The affective roles of Sophia include energetic prophecy (Prov 1:20–33); she "loves, hates, demands, and promises" in the interest of justice, truth, and life.[91] She plays in the new creation, rejoices in God's presence, and delights in humans, renewing their hearts and making them friends of God. "As with Sophia, whoever loves Jesus is beloved by God (John 14:23) and enters into a mutuality so profound that they may be called friends (John 15:15)."[92] Wisdom "fashions all that exists and pervades it with her pure and people–loving Spirit....She is involved in relationships of loving, seeking, and finding with human beings....She is an expression of the most intense divine presence in the world."[93]

As we explore the signs of passion in the mystical works of Hildegard and Hadewijch, we do well to keep in mind the female presence of Sophia. Like Sophia, these women speak an impassioned word, open themselves radically to the shattering presence of God's intense love, and dedicate themselves wholly to lives of virtue. They are women who are not on the sidelines of life, but, like Sophia, they proclaim words of profound connectedness to God, themselves, the church, and the world. We turn now to a Wisdom text that is perhaps the most important for our topic of passion—the Song of Songs.

The Song of Songs

Although our understanding of passion is not limited to sexual metaphors and imagery, the spousal imagery of the Song of Songs is without doubt the primary biblical wellspring for language describing passionate love of God in the mystical tradition.[94] Let us take a moment to examine some of its central images and themes.

The text of the Song of Songs was likely created as a series of ancient love poems or wedding songs in Egypt or Mesopotamia,[95] and then worked and reworked in different cultural settings through many centuries—in Israel, Syria, Greece, Persia. The text includes dialogue between two young lovers and a chorus, perhaps the daughters of Jerusalem. Scholars argue about whether the poem has an underlying unity or sequence or is simply a disparate collection of verses strung together.[96] Also debated are the reasons behind its inclusion in the canon and how it should be interpreted.[97]

Ancient Judaism looked kindly on sexual passion in marriage, viewing it as one of God's many gifts. But the explicitly erotic tone of the Song caused many rabbis to hesitate about its inclusion in the canon, and debate about it reached into the second century CE. In its favor, scholars cite the judgment of Rabbi 'Aqiba (d. 135 CE), who declared that all the ages are not worth the day on which the Song of Songs was given to Israel; for all the Writings are holy, but the Song of Songs is the Holy of Holies. The option to view the Song as an allegory describing the spiritual love of Yahweh for Israel provided the bridge to the Song's official status as revelation. Early Christianity, influenced by the less positive valuation of matter in Greek philosophy, and by Stoic disdain for the passions, also followed this route, seeing the Song as an allegory of love between Christ and the church or Christ and the individual soul. This enabled the Christian community to favor a spiritual interpretation, to transcend the physical dimension of passionate love present in the text.

We have already noted how Origen, the brilliant third–century Christian writer, begins his commentary on the Song by insisting on the mature, spiritual nature of passionate mystical experience. He cautioned that only those who no longer felt the passions of their bodily natures should read the Song. Readers, he says, "must not take anything of what has been said with reference to bodily functions but rather employ them for grasping those divine senses of the inner man."[98] The Greek and Latin fathers most often interpreted the bride in the Song in communal terms, seeing her as the church.[99] Historians note a change of emphasis in the Middle Ages when the bride often refers to the individual monk or nun.

Bernard of Clairvaux offers a similar warning in his sermons on the Song. "Therefore let us not dally outside, lest we seem pre–occupied with the allurements of lust, but listen with modest ears to the sermon on love that is at hand. And when you consider the lovers themselves, think not of a man and a woman but of the Word and the soul."[100] Bernard is well aware of the contours and power of passionate spiritual love. He writes:

65

O strong and burning love, O love urgent and impetu-
ous, which does not allow me to think of anything but
you, you reject all else, you spurn all else but yourself,
you are contented only with yourself! You throw order
into confusion, ignore moderation; you laugh at all
considerations of fitness, reason, modesty and prudence, and tread them underfoot.[101]

But Bernard emphasizes tender rather than passionate love,
since passion is associated with sin rather than grace.

Christian, learn from Christ how you ought to love
Christ. Learn a love that is tender, wise, strong; love
with tenderness, not passion, wisdom, not foolishness,
and strength, lest you become weary and turn away
from the love of the Lord.[102]

As a twelfth–century person, Bernard inaugurated a new
era of reliance on erotic language to speak about encounter with
God. But he obviously would not have been able to acknowledge, name, or celebrate explicitly the range of meanings of passion we have today. Nor could he envision the kinds of positive
links between embodied and spiritual loves we seek.[103] And yet
his own passion is so very obvious to the contemporary reader
who comes to the text without the negative medieval presuppo-
sitions about the body. The exaggerated emphasis on the dangers of lust and sexual passion put us off, and we lament the
silence about the potential value and blessing of intense emotions, and the ways in which human, physical passion and sexual expression are not only valuable in themselves, but can
profitably inform one's spirituality.

There is general agreement that the original setting of the
Song was one of celebration, and no one can deny the erotic
character of the poem. Whether this eroticism should refer
exclusively to the realm of the physical or to the spiritual—or to

both—remains a subject of debate. William Phipps comments that "it is one of the pranks of history that a poem so obviously about hungry passion has caused so much perplexity and has provoked such a plethora of bizarre interpretations."[104] But given the particular historical contexts and worldviews in which this text has been interpreted, it is inadvisable to assign to this rich history the label "bizarre." In fact, we are only now developing a fresh appreciation for allegorical interpretations of the Song of Songs. What is no longer acceptable is to understand the poem *exclusively* in spiritual ways that either ignore or denigrate human sexuality and the intense passionate feelings that attend human, physical, sexual experience.[105]

Let us turn to some examples of the erotic content of the Song. The text of the Song begins with the bride speaking:

> Let him kiss me with the kisses of his mouth!
> For your love is better than wine,
>   your anointing oils are fragrant,
> your name is perfume poured out;
>   therefore the maidens love you.
> Draw me after you, let us make haste.
>   The king has brought me into his chambers.
>   (Song 1:2–4)

The bridegroom responds:

> Ah, you are beautiful, my love;
>   ah, you are beautiful;
>   your eyes are doves.
> Ah, you are beautiful, my beloved, truly lovely.
>   (Song 1:15–16)

The senses of the bridegroom are filled with every detail of the beloved's beauty. He celebrates her beauty with impassioned praise:

You have ravished my heart, my sister, my bride,
   you have ravished my heart with a glance of your
      eyes,
   with one jewel of your necklace.
How sweet is your love, my sister, my bride!
   how much better is your love than wine,
   and the fragrance of your oils than any spice!
Your lips distill nectar, my bride;
   honey and milk are under your tongue;
   the scent of your garments is like the scent of
      Lebanon.
A garden locked is my sister, my bride,
   a garden locked, a fountain sealed. (Song 4:9–12)

In the Middle Ages, the Song of Songs was the most read and commented upon book in the Bible by Jews and Christians alike.[106] Medieval monasticism had inherited from Origen (via Jerome) a threefold schema of the spiritual life based on three books from the wisdom literature—Proverbs, Ecclesiastes, and the Song of Songs. These wisdom writings functioned to instruct persons in the three stages of the spiritual life. Proverbs, for beginners, taught one how to live virtuously. Ecclesiastes, for the more proficient, required that one despise the things of this world as vain and ephemeral. The Song of Songs was for the advanced, instructing those far along on the mystical journey about the ways of love and union with God.[107] As we have seen, it was thought that great personal and spiritual maturity was required before one could read and understand the Song correctly, that is, in its spiritual meaning.

Jean Leclercq explains the popularity of the Song as due to the prominence of an eschatological outlook in monastic circles. Eschewing psychological explanations, Leclercq posits that the monks saw in the Song an expression of intense desire for the fullness of beatitude awaited in eternity. "The Canticle is the poem of the pursuit which is the basis for the whole program of monastic life: *quaerere Deum* [search for God], a pursuit which will reach its end only in eternity but which already obtains fulfillment here in an obscure possession."[108]

For many medieval mystics, the passion of the Song reflected the pure, spiritual, and unsullied quest for God, even though it excluded carnal love. The intense nature of the mystics' encounter with God led them to become passionately caught up in receiving and responding to the touch of God. Use of the erotic love language of the Song of Songs was one apt way for them to express these experiences. While spousal imagery is not the only metaphor used to describe intense relationship with God, it is a privileged one in the Middle Ages. But, as we have seen, the relationship between spiritual passion and human passion was viewed on a hierarchical scale with physical, sexual union at the bottom—a perspective that no longer takes adequate account of contemporary views on the body and sexuality.

However, this hierarchy is not present in the Song itself. William Phipps reminds us that the Song of Songs is the most sensuous book in the Bible and in all of antiquity. It speaks of the joy and constancy of genuine affection. It celebrates a bond that is sweeter than honey and stronger than a lion.[109] It also addresses feelings of loss and desolation when the beloved is absent, leading the lover to rush out and seek what her heart craves. Roland Murphy speaks to the connection between human and divine love in the Song.

> The issue is not so much whether the Song deals with human love as opposed to divine love, as if these were two totally disparate things. It deals with love on various levels, and love belongs to both the human and the divine. If God is love, human sexual love must have some relationship to him; it reflects and partici-

pates in a divine reality. Both levels of love are to be retained in the perspective of the Song.[110]

Dualism works against this holistic vision on two levels. For humans, past distrust of the body prevents us from understanding bodiliness as a gift from God, and central to our becoming saints. But present overexposure of the flesh suggests that spirit has been marginalized, making it easier for us to become voyeurs, exploiting the body as an object. As to divine love, we can never cease exploring the meaning of God's love, as it is expressed in the Song of Songs and, for Christians, in the gesture of the "Word made flesh."

David Carr echoes these sentiments, seeing the Song of Songs as a way to overcome traditional opposition between sexuality and spirituality. The Song, he says, invites us to enter into its world and to imagine our lives as characterized by love, by thinking thoughts of love, feeling the feelings of love, and awakening our senses to the beauty of the world and of the "other," and linking all to God. In our sex–saturated and spiritually empty culture, we need to rekindle our connection with erotic love of each other and of God.[111]

Conclusion

In a world prone to skepticism, quick to joke about love, and easily tempted to sentimentality, connecting with *eros* is no small order. Signs of the need for spiritual passion include indifference, feelings of malaise, lack of direction, and excessive preoccupation with self. Like love songs and poetry, mystical literature calls us to consider living with passionate attention and engagement. It challenges us to develop lively, engaged, and passionate spiritualities and theologies. Perhaps the renewed interest in mysticism since the '60s is a sign of our hunger for depth of living, connection with the divine, and with each other.[112]

Liberation theologians speak constantly of doing theology with "spirit" and communicating it to the world with "spirit."[113] The firmness and spiritedness of theological reflection are signs of the spiritual experience that supports it.[114] Theological spirit means several things. It characterizes a theology that cares about and responds to the crying needs of the world. It is also a theology that is deeply grounded in the Spirit of God, a Spirit of hope and compassionate forgiveness, and a love that binds the world together. I also suggest that living and doing theology with spirit points to affective engagement that is open to conversion and to the transformation of hearts from "stone" to "flesh" (Ezek 36:26). To live with passion is a choice we are free to ignore or embrace.

The words of the Book of Revelation echo throughout the ages: "I know your works; you are neither cold nor hot. I wish that you were either cold or hot. So, because you are lukewarm, and neither cold nor hot, I am about to spit you out of my mouth. For you say, 'I am rich, I have prospered, and I need nothing.' You do not realize that you are wretched, pitiable, poor, blind, and naked" (Rev 3:15–17). These sentiments and this kind of language are echoed in Christian mystical literature and in the lives of the saints from Paul to Dorothy Day. Who is the God behind such words, and who are the people who respond by allowing themselves to get caught up in this web of intense longing and love? Let us turn to Hildegard and Hadewijch.

Chapter 3

Passion in Hildegard of Bingen

*Whoever has knowledge in the Holy Spirit and wings of faith,
let this one not ignore My admonition, but taste it,
embrace it and receive it in his soul.*

Hildegard of Bingen

Introduction

To engage firsthand the role of passion in primary mystical texts, let us turn to the works of Hildegard of Bingen and Hadewijch of Brabant. Our focus is the meaning of religious passion expressed in the language and imagery used to describe their encounter with God, in their theologies, and in manifestations of intense commitment—what might be called their singleness of purpose or purity of heart.

There are several reasons for choosing accounts of medieval women's mystical experience to illustrate the role of passion in the spiritual life. First, since mysticism is an intense form of religious experience, accounts of mystical experience are likely to reveal elements of what passion is and how it functions in the spiritual life.[1] Second, study of the presence and role of passion in accounts by women mystics contributes to a larger historical agenda that seeks to recover all aspects of women's history—including their participation in the highest reaches of mystical union. Such women serve as models and heroines of the Christian life and contributors to Christian theology. Third, it is a commonplace that Western culture has consistently linked affectivity with women. Let us explore this third point further.

In most cultures, women are seen—for good and ill—to be familiar with, and good at, the ways of the heart. On the positive side, women's love has often been seen as superior in its unconditioned and therefore godlike character—"only his mother could love him." Unfortunately, women's unconditional love is too often limited to motherhood, a perspective that, in the end, ill serves both motherhood and other forms of intense, all–encompassing love. On the negative side, the identification of women with affectivity and "uncontrolled" erotic instincts has caused them to be viewed as unreliable, fickle, and incapable of acting judiciously in a crisis or assuming leadership in "high–stakes" human affairs.

The image of women's uncontrolled passions is seared on the Christian imagination. In the Garden of Eden, we are told, Eve's intense desire for knowledge caused her to assent to the serpent's provocative invitation to partake of the fruit of the tree of good and evil—supposedly bringing catastrophe to the entire human race.[2] The pervasive image of Israel, and then the church, as harlot and prostitute lurks in psyches across the Western world. And, under the influence of Gnosticism, from the earliest centuries of Christianity, descriptions of women's journeys to holiness have often involved metaphoric gender transformation. As they advance in virtue, "weak" women become "virile" women—a process that requires, in part, a conquest of the passions.[3] Unfortunately, historical explanations of the prominence of medieval women visionaries frequently point to "some kind of inherent female emotionalism."[4]

Historians have characterized the High Middle Ages as a time of strong emotion, intense longing, fierce passion, and ardent desire. Henry Osborne Taylor, contrasting classical and medieval sensibilities, claimed that medieval Christianity attained "heights and depths of emotion undreamed of by antiquity."[5] I have chosen to reflect on passion in the works of Hildegard of Bingen and Hadewijch of Brabant because they reflect two very different personalities. Hadewijch's descriptions of her encounters with God and with Love are boldly erotic. Her poetry reflects an intensity of passionate experience. Hildegard, on the other hand, tends toward the cerebral. Her elaborate and powerful images are described and explained allegorically with an eye toward understanding. Hildegard presents

Christian teaching on the basis of self—evident truths rather than on textual authority.[6]

Life and Context

Hildegard of Bingen—prophet, scientist, mystic, visionary, poet, dramatist, musician, composer, and theologian—was the quintessential renaissance woman of the twelfth century.[7] Born the youngest of ten children in 1098 to Mechtild and Hildebert von Bermersheim, a Rhenish nobleman, Hildegard spent most of her life in the Rhineland area of Germany. A precocious child, Hildegard began to see visions at a very young age. When she was eight, she was sent as companion and student to Jutta von Spanheim, who was only six years her senior. During an illness, Jutta vowed that if cured, she would become a nun. At age twenty, Jutta joined the Benedictine monastery of St. Disibod. In 1112, she and Hildegard took monastic vows. In 1136 Jutta died, and at thirty—eight Hildegard was elected abbess of the growing group of women religious.

Hildegard's literary output is both prolific and diverse.[8] Her visionary theological triology begins with *Scivias,* completed in 1151, and taking its title from the Latin exhortation, "Know the ways of the Lord." In 1158, she began a second volume on ethics entitled *The Book of Life's Merits (Liber vitae meritorum),* completed in 1163.[9] A third volume, a more scientific treatise written between 1163 and 1173, is titled *On the Activity of God (Liber divinorum operum).* Hildegard also wrote about nature. *A Study of Nature (Physica)* is composed of nine books treating plants, trees, precious stones, animals, and reptiles. *Holistic Healing (Causae et curae)* is a handbook that provides information about illness and healing.[10] She composed liturgical poetry and music for use in her monastery. These songs were later compiled under the title *Symphony of the Harmony of Celestial Revelations (Symphonia harmoniae caelestium revelationum*).[11] Her corpus also includes many shorter occasional works, among them the lives of her patron saints, Rupert and Disibod and 390 letters.[12]

Hildegard's correspondence is impressive, spanning the last three decades of her life.[13] She wrote to popes (Eugene III, Anastasius IV, Adrian IV, and Alexander III); emperors (Conrad III and Frederick Barbarossa); royal families (Henry VI of Germany, Henry II and Queen Eleanor of England, and Queen Bertha of Greece); monks and nuns (Bernard of Clairvaux, Thomas Becket, Elisabeth of Schönau); prelates, and laypersons.[14] She was involved in some of the major political and religious issues of her day—the Crusades, the struggle between empire and papacy, and the Cathar heresy.

Hildegard was acknowledged and revered in her own lifetime, receiving commendations from Pope Eugene III and Bernard of Clairvaux, as well as accolades from laity, monastics, and clergy. In spite of frequent illness, she managed to found two monasteries and completed four arduous preaching journeys later in her life.

Evidence of passion in Hildegard's writings is distinctive and instructive inasmuch as her style impresses the reader as eminently rational, subdued, and orderly. Paradoxically, Hildegard expresses her passion in her dedication to reason. In *On the Activity of God*, Hildegard envisions God as a fire, the very life of the universe, a fire that she sees as rationality itself. "All things are brought into being through this rational light that emanates from God and gives all creatures life" (I.1.9).[15] Hildegard describes her visions primarily in terms of light—a metaphor linked to the mind and insight. She does not allude to ecstatic interludes, rarely addresses God in the second person, and pays little attention to the Song of Songs.[16] In some ways she is the antithesis of her contemporary, Bernard, whose mystical accounts overflow with intense spousal language and imagery. But while Hildegard's work is not marked by apophatic negations or descriptions of nuptial rapture, she clearly communicates a sense of mystery and intense love.[17] Our focus is her doctrinal work, *Scivias*, with occasional references to other writings.

The *Scivias* follows a trinitarian pattern. Part I reflects on the work of God and the ways in which God relates to humanity and to the world. Part II focuses on the Savior and charts the process of redemption. Part III takes as its theme the Holy Spirit, describing especially the role of the virtues in the journey of salvation. The text ends with an apocalyptic vision of the final judgment. Scholars contrast the tone of the *Scivias*, in which Hildegard paints the image of a tumultuous world in flux, with that of *On the Activity of God*, a structured, ordered account of the relations in the universe, in which she presents a more delineated, detailed, and static image of the world, verging on the mathematical.[18] For this reason, the *Scivias* is the best choice for our inquiry. My comments are organized under three general headings: the language, imagery, and symbols of passion; incarnation; and intensity of passion, reflected in action and commitment.[19]

Language, Symbol, and Image

Light

In a first exposure to the *Scivias*, the reader is startled by the detailed imagery with which each vision begins. Brilliant colors abound—red, purple, and green, as well as black and white.[20] The color green, symbol of spiritual and physical health, runs as a leitmotif throughout the text and symbolizes many things: the new spiritual growth and flowering of those who follow the Word (II.6.28; III.10.4 and 7);[21] the freshness of redemption (II.6.26); the color the anti–Christ will remove from the forest

(III.11.27). We will return to Hildegard's use of the color green below in our examination of her lyric descriptions of nature.

The sensuousness of the use of color in Hildegard's texts is juxtaposed with frequent descriptions of light—one of Hildegard's more prominent images. Light is described in varying degrees of shape and intensity and has as many meanings. She begins Part II of the *Scivias* with the following:

> And I, a person not glowing with the strength of strong lions or taught by their inspiration, but a tender and fragile rib imbued with a mystical breath, saw a blazing fire, incomprehensible, inextinguishable, wholly living and wholly Life, with a flame in it the color of the sky, which burned ardently with a gentle breath, and which was as inseparably within the blazing fire as the viscera are within a human being. And I saw that the flame sparked and blazed up. And behold! The atmosphere suddenly rose up in a dark sphere of great magnitude, and that flame hovered over it and gave it one blow after another, which struck sparks from it, until that atmosphere was perfected and so Heaven and earth stood fully formed and resplendent. (II, Prologue)

Images of fire and light most often refer to the deity whom Hildegard consistently discusses in trinitarian terms. She follows the tradition of associating fire with the Holy Spirit and light with the Word. Fire also represents the perfection of those who imitate the Passion of Christ in their burning love (II.5.13).

Her account of the visions challenges readers to become involved with all their senses. Hildegard's descriptions are vivid, sensuous, and intense, beckoning the reader to enter into an all–consuming and passionate relationship with God.

Nature

In addition to the sensuous effect of the use of color and light, Hildegard links the spiritual with the created world through her lyrical descriptions of nature. While one would hardly describe Hildegard as a "romantic," both her environment and her scientific bent caused her to pay close attention to nature's rhythms. Hildegard begins many of her letters by comparing the spiritual life to aspects of nature—bright sun and dark storm clouds, light of day and moon of night, whirlwinds and serene weather.

Images of fire and the green of nature are integrated in her presentation of the Holy Spirit, the trinitarian Person with whom she associates what she calls "greening" (*viriditas*). Hildegard imagined the outpouring of the Spirit in natural rather than cultural metaphors. She combined images of planting, watering, and greening to speak of the presence of the Holy Spirit. Hildegard linked the flow of water on the crops with the love of God that renews the face of the earth, and by extension, the souls of believers.

Scholars explain the prominence of the color green in Hildegard's work in a number of ways, one of which suggests that she may have been influenced by the lush green countryside of the Rhineland Valley. But greenness played a larger role in Hildegard's theology. In the English–language edition of her letters, the translators lament, "This *viriditas*, this despair of translators, this 'greenness' enters into the very fabric of the universe in Hildegard's cosmic scheme of things. In Hildegard's usage it is a profound, immense, dynamically energized term."[22] For Hildegard, *viriditas* expressed and connected the bounty of God, the fertility of nature, and especially the presence of the Holy Spirit. Barbara Newman comments about this aspect of Hildegard's thought, "If you are filled with the Holy Spirit then you are filled with *viriditas*. You are spiritually fertile, you are alive."[23] Hildegard describes the prelate who is filled with weariness *(taedium)* as lacking in *viriditas*, and counsels the neophyte in religious life to strive for "spiritual greenness."[24]

In addition to life and fertility, the *viriditas* of the Spirit points to a life of virtue, the active fruit of the Spirit's gift. The garden where the virtues grow is imbued with *viriditas*, and in a letter to Abbot Kuno, Hildegard describes St. Rupert, a man of exceptional virtue and the patron of her monastery, as the *viriditas digiti Dei*, the "greenness of the finger of God"—a divine spiritual version of a "green thumb"?[25] In one of her many descriptions of the Trinity in the *Scivias*, Hildegard also connects the Holy Sprit with the flowing freshness of sanctity:

> And so these three Persons are in the unity of insepa-
> rable substance; but They are not indistinct among
> themselves. How? He Who begets is the Father; He
> Who is born is the Son; and He Who in eager fresh-
> ness proceeds from the Father and the Son, and sanc-
> tified the waters by moving over their face in the
> likeness of an innocent bird, and streamed with ardent
> heat over the apostles, is the Holy Spirit. (III.7.9)

Like a fallow field, a person with good heart receives the seed of God's word and thus is granted the gifts of the Holy Spirit in superabundance. The person who sometimes accepts and sometimes refuses God's word has some greenness, though "not much," she says. But one who never chooses to hear the word or waken the heart to the admonition of the Holy Spirit dries up and dies completely.[26]

Hildegard employs a coincidence of opposites to describe the sweetness of the Holy Spirit given at confirmation. It is both serene and boundless, swift to encompass all creatures in grace. She continues, "Its path is a torrent, and streams of sanctity flow from it in its bright power, with never a stain of dirt in them; for the Holy Spirit Itself is a burning and shining serenity, which cannot be nullified, and which enkindles ardent virtue so as to put all darkness to flight."[27]

Another example of such nature imagery appears in a letter to Bertha, queen of Greece. Bertha has written to Hildegard for counsel concerning her inability to conceive a child. Hildegard responds to the queen about God's workings in terms of the cycles of nature.

> God's Spirit breathes and speaks: in wintertime, God takes care of the branch that is love. In summer, God causes that same branch to be green and to sprout with blossoms....It is through the little brook springing from stones in the east that other bubbling waters are washed clean, for it flows more swiftly....These lessons also apply to every human being to whom God grants one day of the happiness and the glowing sunrise of glory. Such a person will not be oppressed by the strong north wind with its hateful foes of discord.[28]

Hildegard then turns to imagery of romantic love, counseling the queen to look to the One who moves her, to sigh for the Divine. She closes with a prayer in which she describes God as a lover, intensely desiring to possess the queen as God's loved one: "May God grant you what you desire and what you pray for in your need, the joy of a son. The living eye of God looks on you: it wants to have you and you will live for eternity."[29] The description of the idyllic natural setting links the natural and the spiritual and sets the stage for the more personal love talk that follows.

Erotic Love

It is true that the use of erotic imagery is not prominent in Hildegard's work, but she does turn to such imagery at significant points throughout the text of the *Scivias*. Hildegard ends each vision with a refrain. The visions in Part I end with:

> Therefore, whoever has knowledge in the Holy Spirit and wings of faith, let this one not ignore My admonition, but taste it, embrace it and receive it in his soul.

In Part II, God repeats the following:

> But let the one who sees with watchful eyes and hears with attentive ears welcome with a kiss My mystical words, which proceed from Me Who am life.

And in Part III:

> But let the one who has ears sharp to hear inner meanings ardently love My reflection and pant after My words, and inscribe them in his soul and conscience.

Through the use of the literary technique of refrain, Hildegard continually calls the reader back to the affective and passionate character of the spiritual life. These refrains prevent the reader from getting lost in the complex intellectual machinations of Hildegard's mind. After extended allegorical and theological explanations, she gently calls the reader back to the world of divine and human eros—a world of kissing and panting for the Word of God. We also see a graceful harmony between the language of the head (knowledge, sight, and hearing) and of the heart (kisses and panting), harking back to Origen's development of the spiritual senses.

Hildegard also turns to spousal imagery in her description of the incarnation, which will be treated below, and in her discussion of what she perceives as a massive struggle between the forces of good and evil—a theme that runs throughout the text.[30] She counsels religious women and men to become knights who are to gird themselves "manfully with the sword of God's word."[31] The Beloved is a force that counters evil. "I fly from this Satan, I reject him, and I hold him as an enemy forever, for I desire that Lover Whom I may fervently embrace and joyfully possess in and above all things" (III.6.6).

Spouses and Virgins

For the most part, Hildegard echoes the patristic tradition that interprets the bride as symbol of the church. But in other visions, the bride may represent the Word, the individual soul, virgins, Mary, or personified Wisdom. Hildegard sees the church as an uncorrupted bride betrothed to the most powerful king (II.5.1). Reflecting the common understanding of marriage in her day, Hildegard envisions the church as submissive and obedient to the bridegroom, receiving "from him a gift of fertility and a pact of love for procreating children, and educates them as to their inheritance. So too the Church, joined to the Son of God in the exercise of humility and charity, receives from Him the regeneration of the Spirit and water to save souls and restore life, and sends those souls to Heaven" (II.6.1). In Hildegard's eyes, the church of her day was failing to carry out this duty of mediating salvation to the faithful. The divine voice she hears exhorts the church to be faithful to this responsibility.

> And I heard the voice from Heaven saying to Him:
> "May she, O Son, be your Bride for the restoration of
> My people; may she be a mother to them, regenerat-
> ing souls through the salvation of the Spirit and
> water." (II.6.Prologue)

Imagining the church with various faces, Hildegard sees the church approach the cross and be sprinkled with Christ's blood: "[S]he was joined with Him in happy betrothal and nobly dowered with His body and blood" (II.6.Prologue).

The church's purity depends on the presence of members dedicated to virginity. Hildegard does not escape her era's widespread ambiguity about sexuality. Barbara Newman notes how Hildegard "oscillated between a joyful affirmation of the world and the body and a melancholy horror of the flesh—and its master the devil."[32] One is jarred by Hildegard's "bold, affirmative view of sexual symbolism and a largely negative view of sexual practice."[33] The virgin is to be praised because she seeks the Word rather than an earthly husband. It is sinful for the virgin to love anyone else more than the one to whom she is betrothed (II.5.10–12). The virgin glows like the dawn and burns as the flame of the sun (III.13.7). Often in her writings, Hildegard juxtaposes earthly and heavenly love. Talk about passionate love for God is almost always predicated on one's success in despising the world and the desires of the flesh. The struggle to overcome the latter is pressing and difficult in her eyes.

Hildegard also applies this earthly/heavenly dualism to lay and religious life. In a comparison of the two, Hildegard uses erotic imagery for the latter—one chooses religious over lay life because of the burning desire of one's will and the longing of one's soul (II.5.39). In a general letter directed to the laity, God speaks words of chastisement and exhortation, words antithetical in tone to the lyrical strains of erotic love used to describe religious life. The distinctive role of the layperson is to be a servant of the law. In contrast, God says that religious "embrace Me with the kiss of love when for My sake they leave the world and by climbing the mountain of holiness become My beloved children."[34] In a vision, Hildegard describes the virtue of chastity, a vow taken by religious, in terms of the denial of human love:

[B]y Chastity they start wanting to restrain themselves from the desire of the flesh. For abstinence in the flower of the flesh feels strong, as a young girl who does not want to look on a man nonetheless feels the fire of desire. But Chastity renounces all filth and longs with beautiful desire for her sweet Lover, the sweetest and loveliest odor of all good things, for Whom those who love Him wait in timid beauty of soul. (III.8.24)

For Hildegard, passions turned toward God bespeak the height of religious intimacy. Passions turned toward material reality become a major obstacle to the spiritual life. Thus, Hildegard uses the same erotic imagery to speak of the illicit lure of, and sinful desire for, pleasure (that must be abandoned) as she does to describe the glories of mystical experience in which the lover finds it sweeter to pant for God, the creator of all things (II.5.40). Thus, passionate desire for God is a crucial element of the spiritual life. The spiritual, erotic, sexual experience of panting for the beloved is not to be repressed but directed toward God.

Incarnation

Sensuous language is prominent in Hildegard's description of the incarnation of the Word—a centerpiece of her theology. The Trinity always provides the context for her Christology. In one vision, God says:

> Hence let no person ever forget to invoke Me, the sole God, in these Three Persons, because for this reason I have made Them known to Man, that he may burn more ardently in My love; since it was for love of him that I sent My Son into the world....(II.2.3)

For Hildegard, the holy ancients' faith was but a shadow of what would appear in Jesus: "[A]t the Incarnation of the Son of God, it burst into burning light by the open manifestation of ardent deeds" (III.2.1).[35]

While light points to God, and fire and fervor to the Holy Spirit (III.4.12 and 14), Hildegard reserves the most sensuous imagery for the sending of the incarnate Word. In her description of the incarnation, "sweetness" takes on sensuous overtones: "[T]he Incarnation of His Son dripped with the sweet taste of delight, for in Him the heavenly virtues built many mansions through which humanity can return to the supernal Kingdom, which is darkened by no shadow of death" (II.6.3). This sweetness makes it possible for creatures to return to the heavenly kingdom.

In a letter to Belgian monk Guibert of Gembloux, and his community at Villars, Hildegard comments on verses from the Song of Songs (2:4–5) in reference to the Word made flesh. "The king 'brought me into the cellar of wine, he ordained love in me. Stay me with flowers, comfort me with apples: because I languish with love.'"[36] The Son of God is the true vine that provides the best wine and orders human love. In this same letter, Hildegard also associates the incarnation with intense hunger and thirst for justice. She writes that the Son of God is a "resplendent sun, which illuminates the whole world." The love that Christ ordains in us is a fire, embodied most powerfully in the martyrs, "who poured out their blood for Christ and the true faith flew to celestial desire burning with the inextinguishable fire of love." This same love fills the hearts of the faithful "with the sparks of the true faith, for they hunger and thirst for the justice of God (Matt 5:6) and can never be satiated with it...for He is that love (1 John 4:8) that has "neither beginning or end."[37]

Eucharist

At the eucharistic celebration, the offering of Christ's body and blood is drawn invisibly upward toward God, warmed by the heat of the Divine Majesty.[38] Hildegard writes:

People do not perceive this mystery with their bodily senses; it is as if someone encased a precious unguent in simple bread and dropped a sapphire into wine, and I then changed them into a sweet taste, so that in your mouth, O human, you could not taste the unguent in the bread or the sapphire in the wine, but only in sweetness—as My Son is sweet and mild. (II.6.13)

Hildegard uses the image of anointing to describe one aspect of the incarnation. Christ is anointed with oil, which signifies the "holy humanity" with which he was clothed. This image also refers to the forgiveness of sin brought about by Christ's wounds that are anointed and healed. The sapphire points to Christ's divinity. God's fire causes Christ to be born of the "sweet Virgin" allowing believers to partake in his sweet and delightful body and blood (II.6.13).

Thus, the body and blood of Christ are a source of forgiveness and intoxication with charity for those who are dearest to God. The Eucharist reminds Hildegard of a line from the Song (5.1): "Eat, my friends; drink, and be inebriated, my dearly beloved!" (II.6.21). The function of passion in these "dearest ones" is zealously to refrain from fleshly desires. In turn, God kindles in these souls the strongest virtues.

Intensity of Experience and Commitment

Hildegard held herself to high standards of intellectual and affective intensity in her ministry. She is also intent on leading others to follow her example. She chastises a certain Abbot Adelbert because he does not have "wings to fly" that bear up under duress or "glide in serene weather." She notes that while his heart is not hard, he is "asleep in undisciplined listlessness" that prevents him from attending to God "zealously."[39] In another letter to an abbess, Hildegard counsels her to keep one of her sisters in her heart "with blazing love" and to nourish her with "the milk of consolation."[40] In her own case, Hildegard's passion affects not only her spirit but her body as well.

Bodily Effects

Like most female mystics, Hildegard experienced bodily illness that must have been related to the intensity of her life with God. She was often sick, suffering at least three periods of extended and severe disability. Hildegard reports that illness often appeared when she was prevented from executing what she believed was God's mandate for her. She was told to commit her visions to writing, and until she finally undertook this task, she experienced violent illness. In the Introduction (Declaration) to the *Scivias*, Hildegard writes, "[C]ompelled at last by many illnesses, and by the witness of a certain noble maiden of good conduct and of that man whom I had secretly sought and found...I set my hand to the writing. While I was doing it, I sensed...the deep profundity of scriptural exposition; and, raising myself from illness, by the strength I received, I brought this work to a close—though just barely—in ten years."

A second example of the bodily effects of Hildegard's relationship with God involves her desire to move her convent from St. Disibod to Rupertsberg. The monks at St. Disibod tried to prevent it, fearing the loss of fame and fortune that Hildegard brought to the monastery.[41] She made use of her family connections to secure the support of powerful and wealthy advocates, at the same time taking to bed with a paralyzing sickness that she ascribed to the delay in fulfilling God's will.[42] Hildegard's will to carry out what she thought was God's call brooked no obstacles.

Inner Spiritual Effects

Hildegard's visions obviously produced profound inner effects as well. At the age of seventy–seven, Hildegard writes again to Guibert of Gembloux, describing the spiritual awareness she had experienced since childhood. She calls it her *umbra viventis lucis,* the reflection of the Living Light. In this vision that she saw day and night, her soul rose up into heaven and spread itself out among different peoples who were far away from her in distant lands. She describes the inner effects of her vision of light.[43]

> I can by no means grasp the form of this light, any more than I can stare fully into the sun. And sometimes, though not often, I see another light in that light, and this I have called "the living Light." But I am even less able to explain how I see this light than I am the other one. Suffice it to say that when I do see it, all my sorrow and pain vanish from my memory and I become more like a young girl than an old woman.[44]

Hildegard's visions result in a transformation of self. God's work in her makes her a new creation.

Although Hildegard's ethos is shot through with a sense of struggle, she does not neglect the joy of reward for living a virtuous life. In one vision recorded in the *Scivias,* she sees the joy of the communion of saints. "And in the radiance, which is widely diffused, you see apostles, martyrs, confessors and virgins and many other saints, walking in great joy...who rejoice in the fountain of happiness and the font of salvation, baptized by the Holy Spirit and ardently going from virtue to virtue" (III.4.11). For Hildegard, fidelity to the struggle in the form of a passionate spiritual life bears eternal fruit in intense feelings of joy, thanksgiving, and praise.

Compassion for the Poor

For Hildegard, the ultimate act of illumination is compassion. The compassion of God is to bear fruit in the compassion of the human community for the poor (III.10.26). Toward the conclusion of Part II of the *Scivias*, Hildegard turns to these themes. She counsels her readers to have compassion on those who possess nothing and warns them not to take pride in such activity.[45]

For all the mystics, the passion of their love affair with God extends to others. When passion has its rightful place in human life, one is better able to serve others with compassion, authenticity, and spontaneity. Since the wholeness and truth of God can only be achieved in a shared life, the intimate community of love that passion establishes between God and the soul must bear fruit in the wider community.[46] Hildegard entreats her readers to give to the poor, to divide those material things that "you hold in your bosom and embrace in your heart." She says, "Let your heart's good will overflow, so that you will not be among the lost sheep; sanctify yourself before God by giving of your substance to refresh those in want, and God will give you His mercy in your misery" (II.6.89).

Passion for Virtue

The larger context for care of the poor is Hildegard's passionate concern with the virtues, especially for what she calls "justice." It is difficult to be precise about what Hildegard means by justice, since the term appears on almost every page of her corpus, and she does not offer any systematic explanation of the term. But it seems safe to say that she is influenced by the biblical material on justice and the virtues, as well as by the ways in which this material had been interpreted in the tradition she inherited, especially in the Gregorian reform.

In a letter to a superior who is "limping along in good works," Hildegard paraphrases Psalm 25:2: "[B]urn my reins [refers to the seat of the emotions],[47] which overflow from the sins in which I was conceived, and see that they do not lead me astray…but cause me to be always aflame with the fire of the Holy Spirit, so that I may desire your justice day after day, and ascend from virtue to virtue."[48] She counsels this superior to "kiss God" by purifying his desire through good works and the fear of God.

In other situations, her concern for justice assumes different forms. Toward the end of her life, the prelates of Mainz placed her community under interdict because she had given permission, against their will, for a young excommunicated nobleman to be buried in her monastery's cemetery. The prelates wanted the body exhumed, but Hildegard refused, maintaining that the man had been privately reconciled before he died. Although we may never know the circumstances, nor Hildegard's motivation, we do know that she refused to back down in this struggle with church authorities. The interdict, which denied her community its life blood—Eucharist, communion, and the chanting of the divine office—was lifted only a short time before her death at eighty–one.

Hildegard's passion for justice took on a particular focus in her prophetic activities aimed at correcting abuses in the church of her day: schism, heresy, priests living with concubines, the neglect of preaching, buying and selling religious offices. She is scandalized and outraged by what she sees as the failure of the church to serve its people, to stand up for its true convictions, and to confront those powers in the larger society that Hildegard judges to be evil and destructive of God's plan (III.11.1–42).[49] Barbara Newman describes Hildegard's world:

> While the mighty prelates of Cologne, Mainz, and Trier engaged in political intrigues, supported Frederick's Italian wars, and amassed land and riches for their personal aggrandizement, the church as Hildegard saw it suffered persecution from within. Christ's beleaguered bride appeared in grave distress, like a virgin threatened with rape; her face spattered with dust, her silken robe in tatters, her shoes mired with grime.[50]

In a graphic and stinging use of nature imagery, Hildegard writes to the archbishop of Cologne admonishing him to correct his sinful subordinates rather than imitate their "filthy and unstable ways." She compares them to hogs: "Take note, for example, that hog slop fattens pigs, but if it is mixed in with the fodder given to clean animals that chew the cud, those animals waste away. So it is with you."[51]

And yet, Hildegard's passion for virtue did not prevent her from counseling abbots and abbesses to exercise kindness and mercy in the care of their flocks. Harsh words and severe punishments do not serve to nurture those seeking to grow in the spiritual life. She advocates Benedictine moderation in ascetic practice and discretion in all things, for "through it, the spirit and the body are governed, and they are fed with proper restraint."[52] Hildegard encourages those who seek her help to act in charity not wrath, to become like mothers, full of compassion and sweetness.[53]

As a reformer, she assumes the task of the prophet with passionate intensity. Colloquially, one might say that Hildegard was a "one–tracker," a woman of single vision who did not allow herself to shrink from delivering the prophetic word, nor retreat from the vigorous struggle for good against the powerful forces of evil as she saw them. Earlier in her life, Hildegard expressed a radical trust that the church, the bride of the Word, although weary, would never be destroyed. The renewal would take place in history and be fulfilled in the eschaton. "But at the end of time she will rise up stronger than ever, and become more beautiful and more glorious; and so she will move sweetly and delightfully to the embraces of her Beloved" (III.11.1). But as time wore on, she seemed to view the ecclesial will to reform as both recalcitrant and increasingly anemic.

Significant in her prophetic struggle for reform was the war against heretics, particularly the Cathars, who were present in the Rhineland as early as 1140 and were gaining converts during Hildegard's lifetime.[54] Hildegard blamed clerical laxity for the flourishing of these heresies. Devout laity, sickened by the chaos and moral turpitude of church leaders, turned to the Cathars, who embraced a life of simplicity, poverty, and virtue—an attractive alternative for those serious about Christian discipleship. Hildegard wrote with energy and enthusiasm against Catharist positions: their dualistic cosmology with its disdain for the material world, their rejection of the sacraments and the institutional church, and their view that anything related to sexuality was unclean.[55]

On the level of the individual, Hildegard exhorts persons to lives of intense virtue. She often contrasts true commitment to virtue with the biblical image of being lukewarm. In a well–known passage in the *Scivias*, Hildegard describes a vision in which men and women are carrying vessels of milk and making cheese. The milk represents human seed and the cheese the human beings made from it.

> One part is thick, and from it strong cheeses are made; for that strong semen, which is usefully and well matured and tempered, produces energetic people, to whom brilliant spiritual and bodily gifts are given....And one part is thin...for this semen produces weak people, who are for the most part foolish, languid and useless in their works in the sight of God and the world, not actively seeking God. (I.4.13)

A third group, mixed with corruption, produces bitter cheeses. These are persons whose hearts are filled with bitterness and adversity, and who cannot, therefore, raise their minds to higher things. But God goads them on, forcing them to the path of salvation. Of virgins and celibates, Hildegard says that unless they maintain inner continence of mind as well as the outer continence of the body, they are like "a tepid breeze, with no briskness of heat or cold." They lack the necessary heat in their soul to persevere in the path of virginity that they have undertaken but cannot fulfill (III.10.8).

Once again, we see that Hildegard is not shy about describing in graphic images the ugliness of those whose practice of virtue is tepid and lukewarm. Her aim is to threaten, to cajole, to motivate her readers to strive for the highest reaches of the virtuous life. Because they are endowed with the gifts of intelligence and love, Hildegard encourages anyone who will listen to be passionately committed to virtue. At one point, she explicitly links virtue with the Song of Songs. She writes that the Song is about those who follow the Word, springing forth green and fruitful with the virtues. The sweet and soft Word brings forth holiness and justice (II.6.28). The gifts of intelligence and love are to be put to work to mirror holiness, and thereby to inspire others to be good. The ultimate goal is the praise and glory of God, and gratitude to the Holy Spirit, who is the source and goal of all virtue (III.10.9).

Friendship

One cannot help but wonder about Hildegard's human relationships, given her singleness of purpose as a prophet faithful to God's Word. In general, Hildegard tells us little of her personal feelings toward others, but her letters reveal hints of these relationships.[56] Men, and especially women, monastics write to Hildegard as a cherished friend, and mother, who guides them wisely in the ways of God. Gertrude of Stahleck, aunt of the Emperor Frederick, writes, "I have absolutely no idea what I should write or say to you, for there is no one like you nor anyone so beloved in Christ, and indeed the very strength of my love has destroyed my ability to speak. Indeed, I have become drunk on the wine of sorrow of your absence....I could almost believe it would have been better for me...never to have known your kindness and maternal feeling toward me, for now separated from you by so great a distance, I grieve over you without ceasing as if you were lost to me forever."[57]

Many of her correspondents are grateful to Hildegard for her help and seek her love that functions as a bond across the miles that separate them. An abbess writes, "But since…I cannot fulfill my desire by seeing you in person, I will always see you in my heart and soul, and I will always love you."[58] Hildegard's ability to understand and respond to the problems of her monastic colleagues led many to see her as their spiritual mother.[59] This faithful, tender, and compassionate love stands in contrast to her crusading spirit of reform—both important parts of her highly developed affections.

We do know something about her feelings toward the monk Volmar who functioned as Hildegard's teacher, trusted assistant, and friend for thirty years. In a letter to Abbot Ludwig, she expressed deep love and loss at his death: "Now, like an orphan I toil alone to do God's work, because my helper has been taken away from me, as it pleased God."[60] Hildegard also developed a deep friendship with her scribe and companion, Richardis von Stade. In 1151, Richardis, encouraged by her mother, her brother who was the archbishop of Bremen, and other church dignitaries, accepted the position of abbess of a convent at Bassum. Hildegard violently opposed the move. One wonders if Richardis's family purchased this office for her, or whether the appointment somehow played into the political struggles of Richardis's brother Hartwig, bishop of the diocese of Bremen where the convent in question was located.[61] Either possibility would have enraged Hildegard, who spoke out vociferously against the practice of buying and selling church offices.

In addition, one may conjecture that Hildegard's motives combined deep affection for this woman and disappointment at losing a trusted assistant during a very busy and tumultuous time in her life. In protest, she wrote to ecclesial authorities, and also pleaded with Richardis:

Daughter, listen to me, your mother, speaking to you in the spirit: my grief flies up to heaven. My sorrow is destroying the great confidence and consolation that I once had in mankind....Woe is me, mother, woe is me, daughter, "Why have you forsaken me" like an orphan? (Ps 21:2; Matt 27:46; Mark 15:34). I so loved the nobility of your character, your wisdom, your chastity, your spirit, and indeed every aspect of your life....Now, let all who have grief like mine mourn with me, all who, in the love of God, have had such great love in their hearts and minds for a person—as I had for you—but who was snatched away from them in an instant, as you were from me.[62]

Later, a penitent Richardis decided to return to Hildegard, but Richardis died suddenly, preventing her return.[63] Her brother, the archbishop, wrote to Hildegard to tell her of Richardis's death. Hildegard sent a reply to the archbishop lamenting that while the world loved Richardis's intelligence and beauty, God loved her even more. Hildegard called Richardis "a flower in her beauty and loveliness in the symphony of this world." She continued, "Therefore He [God] was unwilling to give His beloved to a heartless lover, that is, to the world . . . as for me, I cast out of my heart that grief you caused me in the matter of this my daughter."[64] And thus, Hildegard struggles to find peace in the midst of anger and loss.

Conclusion

As might be expected from a holy woman of the twelfth century, Hildegard channeled her passion exclusively toward the spiritual realm. And yet, Hildegard's legacy, taken in the context of her place and time, provides a valuable and compelling expression of passion. Twelfth–century devaluation and even denigration of physical passion was the order of the day, with its attendant exclusion of the laity from the heights of religious experience. But if we leave behind medieval dualisms and monastic elitism, we find in Hildegard a guide to a life of single purpose and passionate commitment to God's ways.

We have seen that Hildegard expresses her intense engagement with God through the creative use of color and light imagery, and through occasional but pointed references to spousal imagery and love. But in the end, her most compelling expressions of passion are intellectual and prophetic in character, oriented toward just action. But Hildegard's obvious passion for acting justly, and her call to others to do likewise, does not obliterate the passive dimension of passionate mystical experience. Hildegard sees herself as a vehicle for God's activity. In a letter to Elisabeth of Schönau, Hildegard says that visionaries and prophets, knowing nothing of heavenly things, "only sing forth God's secrets, like a trumpet that merely gives out sounds, and does not itself labor, but another blows into it, so that it might yield a sound." And she compares her own utterances to "the dim sound of a trumpet from the Living Light."[65]

In a brilliant and creative fashion, Hildegard points the reader toward a holistic understanding of religious experience in which head and heart, action and passion partake in focused orientation toward God. Hildegard's passionate tone challenges the church to renew its own singleness of purpose in the quest for an honest church and a more just world. She leaves no opening for a sentimental love affair not borne out in a virtuous life that includes action on behalf of others.

Hildegard's passion is that of prophet and reformer. She sees sin and evil in vivid ways and is enflamed to confront, to chastise, to encourage, to do battle. The solutions are also painted in vivid tones—she has no patience with excuses and self–justification. Hildegard's passion is also moral, visible through the energy and commitment with which she presents the virtues. At times, her single–minded enthusiasm causes her to sound harsh, but behind the clear call to virtue lies a loving God whose passionate love was expressed in the sending of the Son and Spirit.

An attentive reading of Hildegard forces us to examine the church's responsibility to confront corruption not only in the world, but especially within itself. In a vision of the end of the world, Hildegard describes these sins. She sees the image of a crowned female who represents the church, and at the location of the figure's genitals Hildegard sees a "black and monstrous head" that had fiery eyes, ears like an ass, nostrils and mouth like a lion's. "It opened wide its jowls and terribly clashed its horrible iron–colored teeth."[66] In her love and concern for the spiritual health of the church, Hildegard had the courage to rebuke ecclesial leaders for their greed, laxity, and arrogance. Her honesty about ecclesial failures and her passionate commitment to fight for the integrity of the church can inspire us to follow in her footsteps. Like ecclesial leaders of the twelfth century, leaders today must confront failure in fidelity to the virtues of honesty, openness, humility, repentance, and love for the most vulnerable.

Hildegard's passion can also be described as relational. She saw herself and her sisters as the brides of the Word. In a song in honor of virginity, we encounter Hildegard's most striking example of bridal mysticism:

> Sweet lover! You of the sweet
> embraces! Help us keep
> our virginity.
>
> . . .
>
> We call you now as bridegroom
> for you bought us on the cross:
> we call you to comfort us.
>
> . . .

> O your beauty! O the fragrance
> of the joys we yearn for!
> we sigh for you always,
> banished, weeping –
> when can we see you,
> remain with you?[67]

But she is more concerned with the bride of Christ that is the church. She spent her life committed to its welfare at all levels. She was passionately concerned for the prosperity of her monasteries and those within them, and in a special way for Volmar and Richardis, her dear friends. She spent herself writing letters and traveling to preach in order to assist others on their journey toward God. She dearly desired that all believers be filled with goodness, motivated to act in a loving and just manner, and be on fire with a holy love.

Hildegard ends the *Scivias* in a paean of praise to God. In her final paragraphs she addresses us, her readers, in words overflowing with erotic and sensuous imagery, words that capture the glory of the spiritual life as Hildegard experienced and understood it:

> And whoever tastes this prophecy and fixes it in his memory will become the mountain of myrrh, and of frankincense, and of all aromatical spices, and the diffusion of many blessings; he will ascend like Abraham from blessing to blessing. And the new spouse, the Bride of the Lamb, will take him to herself, for he is a pillar in the sight of God. And the shadow of the hand of the Lord will protect him. (III.13.16)

Chapter 4

Passion in Hadewijch of Brabant

Everything that is yours would be altogether mine;
I should burn to ashes in your fire!

Hadewijch of Brabant

Life and Context

Little is known about Hadewijch of Brabant.[1] Unlike some medieval women mystics whose lives were recorded, we have no "Vita" of Hadewijch. But because her texts contain evidence of her familiarity with chivalry and courtly love,[2] her knowledge of scripture and the fathers of the church, as well as her knowledge of Latin, French, rhetoric, numerology, astronomy, music, and verse, she was probably an educated member of the upper class. Her life and her writing, spanning a twenty–year period between 1220 and 1240, were known in the fourteenth century, but by the sixteenth, her work seems to have been forgotten.[3] She wrote in four genres: *Poems in Stanzas, Poems in Couplets, Visions, and Letters.* In 1838, her corpus was rediscovered by three Belgian scholars.[4] A leading Hadewijch scholar, Paul Mommaers, calls her "the most important exponent of love mysticism and one of the loftiest figures in the Western mystical tradition."[5] Barbara Newman describes Hadewijch as "the greatest mystical poet of the thirteenth century."[6] Bernard McGinn names laywoman Angela of Foligno and the three beguines, Hadewijch, Mechtild of Magdeburg, and Marguerite Porete, as writers who "stand out for the originality of their views and the profundity of their theological vision."[7]

Hadewijch was not a nun, but belonged to a popular and widespread movement of the early thirteenth century whose members called themselves beguines—laywomen who opted for an intentional religious life and whose dwellings were concentrated in the larger towns of Flanders, southern Germany, and northern France—Antwerp, Cologne, Strasbourg, and Bruges.[8]

The beguine lifestyle lay between that of enclosed monastics under perpetual vows and devout laywomen who married. Beguines embraced both a level of withdrawal and of engagement with the world.

The beguine movement began in the late twelfth century and flourished from about 1220 to 1318. It was an extension of the broader religious awakening in the late twelfth and thirteenth centuries that included the foundation of the Franciscan and Dominican orders, with whom the beguines had close contact. Motives for these new forms of religious life included the desire to return to the original purity and enthusiasm of early Christian ideals—prayer, service, and asceticism. While even medieval women in enclosed monasteries had significant contact with the "world," the beguine lifestyle was a distinctive blend of this–worldly and otherworldly values. Some women today have turned to the beguines as a model of a lay vocation that encompasses both a life of prayer and immersion in the affairs of work, family, and social responsibility.[9]

Beguines were often women from the country who moved to urban centers to work, but membership came from various social classes. They lived a loosely structured religious life adapted to different social circumstances and locations.[10] In the beginning, individual beguines lived on their own, but gradually, informally organized groups emerged, and later, more formal beguinages were established. The earliest evidence from 1177 identifies an active beguinage at St. Christophe in Liège, a major center for this form of life. This beguinage occupied an entire neighborhood and numbered more than fifteen–hundred women. In the entire diocese, there are records for at least forty–seven foundations during the thirteenth century.[11] Walter Simons estimates that there were almost three hundred communities of beguines in the Low Countries between 1240 and 1656. He hypothesizes that in the Low Countries in the thirteenth century, life in a beguinage may have been "the most popular of all religious vocations."[12]

Beguines took vows of poverty and chastity for only one year, after which they were free to leave (often to marry). As part of their commitment to beguine life, they promised obedience to a *magistra* or leader chosen from the community.[13] Some women owned and lived in their own homes that might be grouped together in a neighborhood, often near a church. At death or relocation, these homes were sold to other women who wanted to become part of the group. Another architectural form resembled large apartment complexes that could house up to a thousand tenants.[14]

Some beguines begged for alms to support themselves, but more often they worked in schools or hospitals, or earned a living through weaving, nursing, preparing the dead for burial, or working as domestic help. They did not live under any recognized monastic rule, and while they often established relationships with local pastors and bishops, they were not part of any officially recognized institutional structure. As a result, they were often regarded with suspicion and accused of heresy. Another cause for ecclesial concern was the development of mystical vernacular writings by beguines, work that raised questions about authority and orthodoxy.

At the beginning, there was ecclesiastical support. Pope Honorius III expressed approval, and Pope Gregory IV's bull, *Gloriam virginalem*, extended papal protection to "the chaste virgins of Teutonia."[15] But the gradual hardening of church structures in the twelfth and thirteenth centuries put the beguines in jeopardy. Growing hierarchical suspicion of the extreme poverty of the Franciscans, the desire to have more control over lay piety—especially that of women—and the threat of heresy worked against them. The beguines were not without powerful supporters, but they often suffered from the church's fears.

When heresy could not be proven against them, they were often accused of laziness or illicit begging.[16] Several German synods ordered beguines to stop wandering and begging. At church meetings in Magdeburg in 1261, Trier in 1277, and Eichstatt in 1284, beguines were warned against preaching false doctrine. In 1312, at the Council of Vienne, an investigation of beguines and beghards (the name for male groups) was ordered, as well as the dismantling of beguine communities. The council did make allowance for genuinely faithful women to live lives of humility and penance in common, but the opposition signaled the demise of the movement. Some communities responded by adopting the rule of an established order, such as the Cistercians, Dominicans, or Franciscans. A few beguine communities survived well into the twentieth century.[17]

From clues in Hadewijch's writing, we can surmise that she either founded or joined a small group of beguines and then became its leader. Her letters reveal that she believed that the young women in her community were specially called to the mystical state, even though they often failed to live up to her expectations. A number of factors—her high standards, opposition from within and outside of the community, jealousy, and an accusation that she was teaching quietism (a form of prayer that emphasized internal, personal, silent prayer over external observances)—may have led to her being exiled from her community. It is suggested that when she became homeless, she may have offered her services to a leprosarium or hospital for the poor, enabling her to have not only a place to sleep, but also access to a chapel that was usually part of such dwellings in her time.[18]

Love Mysticism

Hadewijch is one of the foremost representatives of *minnemystiek* (love mysticism) to which women made an impressive contribution in the thirteenth century. Barbara Newman suggests that themes of medieval commentaries on The Song of Songs, in which a female human persona relates to a male

Divine Lover, were combined with themes from the courtly tradition of *fin'amour,* in which a male knight courts his "lady," to form a new tradition that she labels *la mystique courtoise.*[19] Bernard McGinn prefers to call this phenomenon "the 'courtly mode' of mystical language," and notes additional characteristics such as the emphasis given to love from afar, the purity and the disinterested nature of love, and the conviction that love of God involved vehemence or violence.[20]

Hadewijch is also significant for Dutch–language literature inasmuch as her *Poems in Stanzas* are among the very few extant Middle Dutch love songs in the troubadour tradition of courtly love. Her prose, along with that of the Cistercian mystic Beatrice of Nazareth (c. 1200–1268), is the earliest extant prose in the vernacular.[21] Hadewijch does not treat love in a systematic fashion, but the word occurs over and over again in her writing and is obviously the controlling concept in her description of the mystical path.

There is some debate about what *love (minne)* means for Hadewijch. Since she infrequently refers to Christ or to bridal imagery, one concludes that Hadewijch understands love as experience rather than as a personification of God or Christ.[22] Hadewijch scholar De Paepe distinguishes three basic moments in Hadewijch's experience of *minne:* the awareness of a distance between *minne* and herself, complete surrender to *minne,* and restored balance. In contrast, Barbara Newman describes Hadewijch's *minne* as real and infinite being, as God, or at least as one potent aspect of God.[23] McGinn rightly comments that the difficulty scholars have in defining *minne* in a clear and precise way is due to the term's richness and provocative ambiguity, emerging as it does out of the complex experience of love as both longing and fulfillment.[24]

As a focus for this study, I have chosen *Poems in Stanzas,* whose forty–five poems reflect the tradition of courtly love—a tradition replete with the passionate and stormy engagement of lovers.[25] Vanderauwera underlines the presence of these themes: "The imagery of courtly love—the unattainable lover, the submissive service to love, the complaints, the hope and despair, the all–pervading power of love—provide the poems with a strong thematic link."[26] But, as we will discover, this literary imagery takes on a new and existential spiritual significance in Hadewijch. The "lady" in the courtly love tradition becomes God or Love to whom the soul offers the service of love. At times, Hadewijch becomes the knight errant, courting dangers and adventures for Love's sake. Mommaers calls these poems mystical love lyrics—a new genre created by Hadewijch and characterized by lyrical genius.[27] In addition, the impact of romance on this type of poetry is well established, making it apt for our inquiry.[28]

We examine Hadewijch's love poetry under five headings: desire; the relation of passion to reason; her emphasis on the humanity of Jesus; the pain involved in passionate love; the effects of passionate love—the transformed self. Since readers may be less familiar with Hadewijch's poetry, I cite a wider range of texts than was the case with Hildegard, to whom readers may have more access.

Desire

Hadewijch is another figure in the long line of spiritual writers who build on Origen's exposition of the "spiritual senses." The use of spiritual senses adds sensuous and erotic tones to the mystics' longing for God. Mystics not only "see" God, they also hear, smell, taste, and touch God as well. Mystical desire is often expressed in terms of hunger and thirst for God (11.5; 14.13). Hadewijch thinks highly of those who continue to want God even when God does not appear: "They who live in hunger for Love / And yet lack fruition / O who can praise them enough?" (15.3). Hadewijch's Poem 33 is titled "Hunger for Love."

For the perfect man it would be a pity
If he, by the counsel of baseborn aliens,
Ceased to perform those noble deeds,
Which create hunger in new satisfaction.

Inseparable satiety and hunger
Are the appanage of lavish Love,
As is ever well known by those
Whom Love has touched by herself.

Satiety: for Love comes, and they cannot bear her;
Hunger: for she withdraws, and they complain....

How does Love's coming satiate?
Filled with wonder, we taste what she is....

How does Love's refusal create hunger?
Because we cannot come at what we wish to know
Or enjoy what we desire:
That increases our hunger over and over. (33.6–10)

Hadewijch characterizes her search for the taste of God as light and sweet. The one who wants to receive "all" from Love must seek Her gladly (28.2).

What is this light burden of Love
And this sweet–tasting yoke?
It is the noble load of the spirit,
With which Love touches the loving soul
And unites it to her with one will.
And with one being, without reversal.
The depth of desire pours out continually,
   And Love drinks all that outpouring.
The debt Love summons love to pay
   Is more than any mind can grasp. (12.3)

In a startling metaphor, Love drinks Hadewijch's desire. But no matter what Love offers, it is never the totality of what there is to give, so the soul's hunger remains (6.6).

More often, though, desire is described as painful, fiery, and violent (4.2; 6.1; 7.5; 22.6; 24.2) and is linked with loss of self.

> To be reduced to nothingness in Love
> Is the most desirable thing I know. . . .
> And if anyone then dares to fight Love with longing
> Wholly without heart and without mind,
> And Love encounters this longing with her longing:
> That is the force by which we conquer Love. (38.7)

The one who seeks union with Love must first taste sour bitterness (17.13). To the reader, Hadewijch's seemingly intense and almost driven personality leads her into a passionate search for God that brooks no obstacles. But her intense longing for God inevitably brings frustration, pain, and disappointment. We may well ask whether she sets her sights too high. On the other hand, we might admire her singleness of purpose, her willingness to risk all in order to attain what she saw as the "pearl of great price."

Her words may also provoke us to reflect on the flame of our own desires for God/the Good. How do we tend the fire of our human longing, our spiritual desires? We can reduce the oxygen and starve it, keep it steady with kindling, splash water on it to put it out, or turn it into a roaring blaze. In her poetry, Hadewijch works hard to get us to choose the blaze.

Love and Reason

Although one is almost overwhelmed by the intense, erotic tone of Hadewijch's writing (in stark contrast to Hildegard), she does not disdain reason. She describes reason as noble, as that part of a person that is renewed and enlightened as a result of ecstatic, affective, mystical experience.[29] Reason has the all–important function of keeping one's eyes on the truth. "Thunder is the fearful voice of threat...and it is enlightened reason which holds before us the truth, and our debt...and our smallness compared to Love's greatness" (Letter 30). The paradigm for the inclusion of both love and reason is the Trinity. Reason, motivating one to perfection, reflects the Son; the will of Love that leads one to exercise the virtues ardently belongs to the Spirit; the drive to imitate God in every way is connected to the Father (Letter 30).

Hadewijch is not naïve about the possible risk to Love that Reason can bring, but she knows that Love without Reason is incomplete (30.9). As a rule, hedonistic persons are not prone to consult Reason, preferring to abandon themselves completely to pleasure. But pleasure is but one aspect of Love. Love literature of all types reports that after promising marvelous things and bestowing initial joy, Love can withdraw, leaving the lover abandoned and alone. Further, Reason reminds Hadewijch that she is a human being and therefore not capable of experiencing the fullness of Love for which she hungers so intensely. At first, she thinks Reason is perversely picking a fight with her, but then she realizes that it was Reason who taught her to live the truth (30.11). Reason also has a key role in the process of discernment, so important to the spiritual life (Letter 24). Hadewijch places her experience of mystical love within the context of truth and the totality of the human person. A love cordoned off from the other aspects of her existence cannot be authentic.

Above all, Reason brings understanding to the experience of passion (9.9). Reason illuminates the entire abyss of Love and gives its approval and counsel to scrutinize, with Love, the whole garden of Love (19.5). Reason safeguards Hadewijch's love affair with God from being closed in on itself. Reason leads her to see the point, the goal of Love. "For no one can become perfect in Love unless he is subject to his reason" (Letter 13).

She knows that even though Reason has a separate function, passionate love is incomplete without it. Reason makes it possible to receive the completion or the fruition of Love, and also *to know* how this is in fact so (30.14). Hadewijch does not covet this discovery for herself. She knows that it is a gift and prays that all those who love might win the favor of Reason. She says:

> In winning the favor of Love
> Lies for us the whole perfection of Love. (30.15)

The pearl of great price is Love, but Love without Reason is ripe for deception.

Hadewijch also acknowledges that Reason is not infallible. It too is subject to error, and when it errs the results are far-reaching. The will becomes weak and lazy; the memory loses its deep notions, its joyous confidence, and its zeal for good action. The noble soul becomes depressed, requiring it to obtain its consolation from bare hope (Letter 4). Hadewijch's heart doesn't really care much for detours, but she does not ignore the tension she feels between the two powers and their differing objectives. But rather than sacrifice one or the other for a false peace, she knows she must allow both to have a say.

> The loving soul wants Love wholly, without delay;
> It wishes at all hours to delight in sweetness,
>   In opulence according to its desire.
> Reason commands it to wait until it is prepared;
> But liberty wishes to lead it instantly
>   Where it will become one with the Beloved.
>   Storms of this kind
>   Impart a calm resignation. (15.5)

It is agony for the passionate soul to wait, and Hadewijch finds the counsel of Reason cruel and confusing (16.3). She is relentlessly honest in describing the full range, and at times, the conflicting aspects of her experience of Love.

Hadewijch offers a powerful and compelling poetic summary of the way she understands the relationship between Love and Reason. I will allow her to speak in her own words:

> The power of sight that is created as natural to the soul is charity. This power of sight has two eyes, love and reason. Reason cannot see God except in what he is not; love rests not except in what he is. Reason has its secure paths, by which it proceeds. Love experiences failure, but failure advances it more than reason. Reason advances toward what God is, by means of what God is not. Love sets aside what God is not and rejoices that it fails in what God is. Reason has more satisfaction than love, but love has more sweetness of bliss than reason. These two, however, are of great mutual help one to the other; for reason instructs love, and love enlightens reason. When reason abandons itself to love's wish, and love consents to be forced and held within the bounds of reason, they can accomplish a very great work. This no one can learn except by experience. (Letter 18)

This text testifies to Hadewijch's penetrating awareness of the distinctive functions of Reason and Love. And her use of charity as the sight that unites these two eyes of the soul is striking in its originality and theological import.

Finally, no matter how great her disappointment at Love, and no matter how deeply Reason has wounded her, she does not abandon the path of passionate attachment to Love. The setbacks do not lead her to close herself off from the experience of passion, but in a way, increase her resolve to continue on this path. She says:

No matter how Love has disappointed me,
I must yet follow her,
For she has utterly engulfed
   My soul, from the depths of my heart.
I will follow her totally. (30.13)

Hadewijch has the courage to persevere in the midst of difficulties. She admits forthrightly that Love enflames her whole being and calls her to be faithful.

Depending on one's historical perspective or particular personality structure, one may favor reason or intense love. It is true that passion without order rightly causes social and religious suspicion. But it is also true that passionate love deserves attention and appreciation. The point is not to celebrate one at the expense of the other. For it is the whole person who lives and loves and thinks and makes decisions. Hadewijch was ahead of her time both in the freedom with which she embraced and talked about passionate love of God, and in her understanding that passion need not be cooled or distorted by reason.

The Humanity of Jesus

Hadewijch's passionate engagement with God is also visible in her Christology, especially in her portrait of Jesus' humanity and the role she assigns to the emotions. Hadewijch's writing resounds with the conviction that mystical union with God is lived not only in heaven, but also here on earth. Since she does not often speak of Christ in *Poems in Stanzas*, we turn to her *Letters* and *Visions* to discover the role of Christ in her mystical experience.

Throughout these writings, Hadewijch speaks consistently of God in trinitarian terms, and within that context, Christ is given a distinctive role. When Hadewijch speaks of union with God, she almost always means the God–man, with Christ's humanity in the forefront.[30] Of all the mystics, Hadewijch conveys most graphically that, beyond a doubt, her experience of Christ is with the male human person, Jesus.[31] Further, her descriptions underline the passionate nature of her love affair with the God–man. Without conformity to Christ's humanity, conformity to the divinity is not possible.

As we will see below, Hadewijch sees conformity to Christ's humanity as the motive force behind leading a virtuous life.[32] She exhorts her readers "to live Christ" in the fullest sense, participating with the totality of their being in the totality of Christ. Each mystery of Christ's life—annunciation, nativity, flight into Egypt, pain, poverty, ignominy, being forsaken yet remaining compassionate—is an invitation to imitate him in his humanity, to enter into comparable experiences in our own lives. But she refuses to let go of either the divine or the human aspects. The truth of both is found in a single fruition. This unity is evident in many of her descriptive passages. For example, in Vision 7, she says:

> I desired to have full fruition of my Beloved, and to understand and taste him to the full. I desired that his Humanity should to the fullest extent be one in fruition with my humanity, and mine then should hold its stand and be strong enough to enter into perfection until I content him, who is perfection itself, by purity and unity, and in all things to content him fully in every virtue. To that end I wished he might content me interiorly with his Godhead in one spirit and that for me he should be all that he is, without withholding anything from me.[33]

For many medieval women mystics, the occasion for such intimate union with Christ was the reception of communion during the eucharistic celebration. Also in Vision 7, Hadewijch offers this powerful erotic description of her experience of union:

With that he came in the form and clothing of a Man, as he was on the day when he gave us his Body for the first time; looking like Human Being and a Man, wonderful and beautiful, and with glorious face, he came to me as humbly as anyone who wholly belongs to another. Then he gave himself to me in the shape of the Sacrament....After that he came himself to me, took me entirely in his arms, and pressed me to him; and all my members felt his in full felicity, in accordance with the desire of my heart and my humanity. So I was outwardly satisfied and fully transported.[34]

After a short while, Hadewijch loses sight of the outward manly beauty and begins to merge with her Beloved. "Then it was to me as if we were one without difference."

At all stages of the love relationship, Hadewijch speaks of her desire to "content" the Beloved.

What I most desired,
Since Love first touched my heart,
Was to content her
According to her wish. (*Poems in Stanzas*, 16.9)

Hadewijch's poetic discourse conveys how her entire being aches to please the Beloved. Persons in love understand this desire. In all forms of intense love, the lover wants nothing more than to have the beloved enjoy whatever gives her/him happiness. In turn, the lover experiences great joy when he is able to content the loved one. And yet in Hadewijch's experience with God, she understands clearly that

No living man under the sun
Can content Love. (20.1)

But this truth does not cool the flame of her love. She has been captured by love and ultimately gives in willingly to its demands in spite of doubt and suffering.

We close this discussion of Hadewijch's account of her relationship with the man Jesus with several stanzas from Poem 20, which describes the sublime nature of love. These stanzas represent the high emotion in Hadewijch's description of her love affair with God.

> God, who created all things
> And who, above all, is particularly Love,
> I supplicate to consent,
>   According to his pleasure,
> That Love now draw the loving soul to herself
>   In the closest union possible to Love.
>
> The union possible to Love is very close,
> But how close, I am the one who does not under-
>   stand.
> But he who is ardent for the sake of Love
>   Shall yet understand
> How Love is always possessed in violent longing:
>   Here one cannot find repose
>   . . .
>
> All who love must be moved to pity
> That Love lets me moan thus
> And cry so often: "Woe is me!"
>   In what season and when
> Will Love reach out to me
>   And say: "Let your grief cease"?
>   "I will cherish you;
> I am what I was in times past;
> Now fall into my arms,
> And taste my rich teaching!" (20.5–6, 12)

The desire for Love is intense and persistent. Even in the midst of severe pain, suffering, and violent longing, Hadewijch perseveres. In the midst of the turmoil, she hears the clear voice of Godly assurance—"I will cherish you...fall into my arms." She portrays an important dimension of the complex experience of passionate love accurately, poetically, and with great feeling. She is obviously deeply immersed in the experience of Love and yet is able to find language that brings to life for others this most intimate of encounters with God.

The Wound of Love

The line from the Song of Songs, "I am faint with love" (2:5), has spawned a rich interpretive history in the tradition of Christian mysticism. We explore how Hadewijch employs the metaphor of the wound of love (now often reduced in the popular imagination to the activity of Cupid on Valentine's Day), and its associations with the pain and suffering of love. Once again, Origen is a primary source for this mystical theme. He wrote:

> If there is ever anyone who at any time has burned with this faithful love for the Word of God; if there is anyone who, as the Prophet says, has received the sweet wound of him who is the "chosen dart"; if there is anyone who has been pierced with the lovable spear of his knowledge, so that he sighs and longs for him day and night, is able to speak of nothing else...and is...not disposed to desire, seek, or hope for anything other than him; then such a soul truly says, "I have been wounded with love."[35]

Hadewijch develops this image when she acknowledges that the pleasures and promises of Love are not enjoyed without cost. She laments:

As Love's arrows strike it
   It shudders that it lives.
At all times when the arrow strikes
It increases the wound and brings torment.
All who love know well
   That these must ever be one:
Sweetness or pain, or both together,
   Tempestuous before the countenance of Love
   . . .
Longing keeps the wound open and undressed
Because Love stormily inflames them. (14.2–3, 12)

Pain, wounding, imprisonment, violence, and despair dot the landscape of Hadewijch's love affair with God.

He who serves Love has a hard adventure
Before he knows Love's mode of action,
   Before he is fully loved by her.
   He tastes her as bitter and sour;
   He cannot rest for an instant. (2.4)

Love has a fickle side. At times, Love gives consolation and health; at other times, Love administers heavy blows and wounds (3.5). The theme of pain and joy intermingled (3.6), so common in the literature of passionate love, runs like a leitmotif throughout Hadewijch's poetry. Truth is revealed in "sweet pain" (12.4); exile is sweet (9.3); and she lives "with a sad heart, joyful" (13.1). In the mode of courtly literature, being in love is also an imprisonment. However, brave knights "ever serve in the chains of Love" (10.3), and Love makes even imprisonment sweet.

That is mighty Love's mode of action:
If she wholly lures someone to her hand,

Although she forces him with violence,
She contents him and sweetens his chains. (19.11)

The lovers mutually conquer each other. In Poem 40,
Hadewijch assumes a male persona.

When he experiences this sweet Love,
He is wounded with her wounds;
When in amazement he beholds her wonders,
He imbibes eagerly from Love's deep veins,
With continual thirst for a new beginning,
Until he enjoys sweet Love. (40.5)

Love initially sweeps Hadewijch off her feet and then withdraws, hiding Herself. This feeling of abandonment by Love
may be connected with Hadewijch's being rejected by her community and left to wander in exile. One of her keenest sufferings
is that of feeling like an alien, an exile in her own land (4.9). In
other instances she speaks of her oppressors, perhaps her
once–loving sisters, as aliens. She is puzzled and worn down by
all her grief. She says:

So greatly has the pain of love worn me out
That I am now unfit for anything. (2.8)

In her talk about exile, Hadewijch recapitulates a medieval theological worldview that saw the world as coming forth from
God (*exitus*) and returning to God (*reditus*). This Christianized
view of a Neoplatonic theme claims that since humanity's true
home is in God, the time between coming forth and returning
to one's true home is experienced as exile, as being in a foreign
land. Augustine writes eloquently about longing for "the father-
land," for the peace and harmony of heaven. Hadewijch's personal history and personality may have caused her to embellish

the experience of exile, leading her to express this traditional theme in strikingly dramatic ways.

Hadewijch is puzzled by what she perceives to be the intense agony of her lot. She does not record the suffering due to the ordinary round of upsets and discontents, but rather that of monumental pain. These experiences reflect a violence rarely spoken of so directly in mystical literature. She says:

> O what did I do to good fortune
> That it was always so merciless to me?
> That to me it did such violence—
> More than to a thousand other souls? (3.2)

Again, turning to imagery of the courtly love traditions, Hadewijch laments that her shield has warded off so many blows that there is no room left for even one more gash (3.3). Even her longing for love takes on violent dimensions.

> The union possible to Love is very close,
> But how close, I am the one who does not under-
> stand.
> But he who is ardent for the sake of Love
> Shall yet understand
> How Love is always possessed in violent longing:
> Here one cannot find repose. (20.6)

She wishes that she could understand her "losses, defamations and oppressions" as good, but she does not have the wisdom (3.4).

At moments, Hadewijch seems near despair, but she clings to her vision. She often turns to paradox as she struggles to express the intensity and complexity of her encounter with Love.

> We must wholly forsake love for Love;
> He who forsakes love for Love is wise.

It is all one whether we die or live:
To die for Love's sake is to have lived enough.
Alas, Love! You have driven me to extremity:
But in this very extremity to which you have driven
    me,
I will keep vigil, Love, in service of your love.
    (43.14)

In the long run, Love is faithful to Hadewijch. She suffers gladly knowing that Love has never revoked her promises (2.8). "However cruelly I am wounded / What Love has promised me/ Remains irrevocably" (16.10). Love honors her friends and can be counted on even though she causes "smarting pain" (2.10). Hadewijch will "endure Love's storms with confidence" (2.11).

The deep suffering that Hadewijch describes is an inescapable component of her passionate love affair with Love. Although historical evidence is inconclusive, one may surmise that her descriptions of spiritual pain are connected with the rejection and suffering she knew in her lifetime. Her one–track mentality may not have permitted her any compromise, and as a result, her life takes on a literal imitation of Christ, who, the gospels tell us, had nowhere to lay his head (Matt 8:20; Luke 9:58). Her life is thus characterized as passionate, not only in her dedication to God, but also in the painful consequences of that commitment.

But at a more profound level, one can reflect on the inevitable onslaught of suffering experienced whenever one chooses to become vulnerable, to open oneself to the gift of passionate love. Human experience opens a window onto this type of engagement with God. In addition to the joyful wounding of the love experience in itself, there are other sources of pain. The "other" is given permission to enter deeply into the lover's psyche. This entrance requires revelations of self and often painful adjustments to accommodate the other. One also allows oneself to become intensely caught up in the beloved's affairs. This creates another kind of vulnerability that opens one to being wounded. The stance of passion is never the distant, cool, safe position of the disinterested onlooker. Lovers become united in a way that causes the pain and suffering of one to be felt deeply by the other. Often the most painful form of suffering occurs when one is unable to relieve the suffering of the beloved. Then, love leads to the generous desire to assume the suffering oneself.

Hadewijch witnesses to a love that perseveres in spite of intense suffering. She is not timid about her lamentations—one is reminded of the pathos of the psalms of lament in the Hebrew scriptures—but the flame of her desire is not dimmed by hardship. The vision of her beloved Love and the promise of joyful fulfillment are always before her, leading her on and giving her strength in the midst of adversity.

Nature Imagery

In the spirit of the troubadours, Hadewijch deftly weaves the symbols of nature and the seasons throughout her tale of love. Much more prominently than Hildegard, Hadewijch returns again and again to the rhythms of nature. Her graphic depiction of the renewal of nature points to the many levels of renewal of her deeply human spiritual life. Hadewijch keeps her eye on the promise of spring. Days grow longer; hazelnut trees blossom; sap flows upward from the roots; meadow and plant don their foliage; birds grow joyful and sing; roses appear between thorns; flowers open wide and take on transforming color; storms give way to fair weather.

But nature, like love, can be fickle. Winter is harsh and brings a heavy heart (43.1). Even a new springtime and new Love can "[s]trike together one single wound." Hadewijch's fresh experience of spring wounds her heart anew—"That this noble being / Remains hidden from us / In her subtle nature such a long time" (18.3). But in the end, trust and hope win out. In Poem 7, she writes:

125

> Oh, Love is ever new,
> And she revives everyday!
> Those who renew themselves she causes
>   to be born again
> To continual new acts of goodness.
> How, alas, can anyone
> Remain old, fainthearted at Love's presence?
> Such a person lives truly old in sadness,
> Always with little profit;
> For he has lost sight of the new path,
> And he is denied the newness
> That lies in new service of Love,
> In the nature of the love of new lovers. (7.3)

In the midst of her anguish, Hadewijch experiences spring as promise, and trusts that her own renewal will emerge as tangibly as the renewal of nature each year. But on occasion, the reader also glimpses hints of a renewal that is already realized.

> The new year already begins.
> For anyone who has resolved
> To spare neither much nor little
> For Love, his pain becomes pure profit. (33.2)

In another vein, she prays that others may also know new life.

> May new light give you new ardor;
> New works, new delights to the full;
> New assaults of Love, new hunger so vast
> That new Love may devour new eternity! (33.14)

Hadewijch's lyrics bring nature to life as sign and symbol of the renewal that divine love promises. For her, nature serves as troth from the Lord. Her response is to trust in God's fidelity.

The Transformed Self

We come now to the final and most important aspect of Hadewijch's passionate love affair with God—the transforming effects wrought in her. The proof of authenticity in the spiritual life is the quality of life that flows from it. As one becomes more deeply attuned to "life in Christ," the dispositions, choices, and activities of life increasingly reflect the life of the Beloved. Such actions are grounded in the new identity that emerges from a passionate encounter with God. In a very real sense, one becomes and continues to become a new person, a new creation.

The call of passion occurs at different stages of one's life. Recent psychological analysis of the stages of life suggests that passion is more likely to knock on one's door at certain pressure points along life's continuum, for example, in adolescence or midlife. At certain moments, one may discover one's potential for passionate engagement; at others, one may need to rekindle the flame of passionate living that has been allowed to flicker or even go out. But reflection on the complexity and diversity of human life leads to the acknowledgement that the call of passion can occur at any time and in any circumstance. It can be called forth by a person, an object, or an idea. Christians are mindful that behind the lure of passion lies a God of passionate love, who calls to the seeker in unique and often surprising ways, and is the condition for the possibility of a similarly passionate response.

Too many of us are probably too busy and distracted even to recognize the knock when it occurs. Others suppress the call quickly for a variety of reasons—fear, or perhaps just inconvenience. Yet others will do battle with passion. Outcomes vary. One may succeed in overcoming the drive toward passion, or passion may be the victor in a harmful way, leading toward misery and destruction. Rosemary Haughton contends that it is not possible simply to reject the call and go on as before.[36] The defenses one has built up must either be strengthened or abandoned. In the first instance, prejudices and habits of thought that were taken lightly must assume the force of fixed immovable truths in order to be strong enough to repel the invasion of passion. Hadewijch says of this option:

> All who shun this renewal
> And renew themselves with newness not that of
>   Love
> Shall be distrusted by the new,
> And condemned by both the new and the newly
>   reborn. (7.7)

In a second option, one opens oneself to the self–knowledge and integrating power that the experience of passion makes available. Hadewijch was not afraid to open the door to passion and to allow its searing power to work in her. The fruit is a more profoundly human and holy person. We have had a glimpse of the ways in which passion becomes a thread woven throughout her poetry. Here is a particularly powerful example:

> Oh, how sweet is proclaiming the renewal!
> Although it occasions new vicissitudes
> And many new sufferings,
> It is a new security;
> For love will truly repay us
> With great new honors;
> Love shall cause us to ascend
> To Love's highest mystery.
> Where that new totality shall be
> In glorious fruition,
> And we shall say, "New Love is wholly mine!"
> Alas, this newness happens too seldom! (7.7)

We discuss the textual evidence for Hadewijch's transformation under the following themes: her use of nature imagery, the experience of surrender, the virtuous life, her joy and optimism.

Surrender

A passionate spirituality is not automatic or magical, but depends on the choice to abandon oneself to its power. It is obvious that Hadewijch chose to surrender herself to Love. But given the ways in which surrender is proposed to women by church and society—often to their detriment—we must treat this theme with critical caution.

Contemporary feminist scholarship warns against naïve or precipitous surrender. Culturally, surrender has been associated with women—one might even say that culture has "assigned" surrender to women in a distinctive way. In particular, the sexual act is understood paradigmatically as one in which men are agents of initiation, and women surrender passively. But the genuine problems for women inherent in any discussion about surrender must not blind us to its positive role in human and religious experience, provided it is a free choice on the road to holiness. The essence of the Christian story involves laying down one's life in love and freedom for another. But it is critically important that women especially understand the complexities and nuances of this act, making sure that the prior work involved in "having a life" and being free is well underway. One must have a life in order to surrender it.

Hadewijch is clear about her choice to surrender to Love's demands. She says:

> Alas, I gave full trust to Love,
> Since first I heard her named,
> And I left myself to her free power. (1.4)

In fact, in her mind, this choice is the very reason why everyone around her wishes to condemn her. She defers to Love, makes herself continually available to Love (36.2), trusting that Love is wise and knows best—whether Love's decision is to scourge or pardon (1.6, 8). Clearly this is advice that can stand up only when the love in question is the love of God.[37] Hadewijch prays that Love dispose of her freely according to Her pleasure (2.9; 3.2):

> I do not complain of suffering for Love:
> It becomes me always to submit to her,
> Whether she commands in storm or in stillness.
>   (22.4)

Whether postmodern women are able to cross over sympathetically into the courtly world Hadewijch occupies, at the least, we can acknowledge and admire her willingness to risk speaking of her experience of radical loss of self with honesty and abandon:

> This is the best counsel
>   That can be given on the subject:
>   To one whom Love has thus captured
>   And bound with her chains,
>   That he surrender himself into her hands
>   And always be submissive
> To all the lordship that Love exercises:
>   . . .
>
>   Love has subjugated me:
>   To me this is no surprise,
>   For she is strong and I am weak.
>   She makes me
>   Unfree of myself,
>   Continually against my will.
> She does with me what she wishes;

Nothing of myself remains to me;
   Formerly I was rich,
Now I am poor: everything is lost in love. (24.4–5)

Hadewijch places before the reader the terror of passionate love. The risk of loss of self is real, and one is foolhardy to ignore the seriousness of the stakes that are involved.

Perhaps we can listen to Hadewijch in a new key. For example, what might it mean today to surrender oneself, to give oneself over fully to *life* in freedom? Does not *life* demand a kind of surrender? Does not *life* demand constant conversion in the midst of its slings and arrows? In the spiritual life, loss of the old self is a sine qua non of the emergence of the new. In her exile, Hadewijch finds a way to live freely and receive grace and knowledge from Love. She is very sure of herself here. She says:

He who disputes them with me has it on his con-
   science.
I cannot do without this gift,
I have nothing else: I must live on Love. (24.6)

Surrender has further dimensions to it. It results, paradoxically, in the empowerment of the lover. The one who in her youth is wholly submissive to Love, and who is strong in virtue, ends up receiving in full freedom "Love's unheard–of power." In turn, this power allows the lover to "subdue Love / And be her lord and master" (6.4). Hadewijch writes:

For I understand from the nobility of my soul
That in suffering for sublime Love, I conquer.
   I will therefore gladly surrender myself
   In pain, in repose, in dying, in living. (22.2)

Hadewijch describes herself as taking a persistent stand against Love, a move that results, not in being overcome, but in becom-

ing as strong as Love. She continues with the ambiguous suggestion that Holy Church invites all who are docile to take such an
empowering stand against Love, and she ends the stanza with
"May God now come to our assistance!" (23.8). Love is con-
quered by the force of mutual longing with which one must dare
to fight.

Any genuine spiritual life involves struggle—from Jacob's
wrestling with the angel to Martin Luther King.[38] People struggle with God's call to vocation, to love, to justice. They do not
simply roll over at the first sound of God's voice. But because of
love, they engage. The lover seeks Love in both resistance and
gladness, and like Hadewijch, is willing to brave any obstacle,
even death, if she wishes to receive Love. When Love commands, the lover must be ready to act boldly and to carry out
Love's wishes (28.2; 39.4).

Life of Virtue

Hadewijch follows in the footsteps of Hildegard in her
emphasis on a life of virtue. Along with the freedom to choose
Love, virtue is the most visible fruit of a love affair with God,
and Hadewijch speaks of it with great passion—in the form of
commitment. The specific virtues of courtly love play a major
role in Hadewijch's description of the spiritual life. Fidelity has
a leading role. Love is characterized by unwavering faithfulness,
and Hadewijch is repeatedly counseling the soul to remain
faithful to Love, no matter how difficult and painful. In the
courtly tradition, a knight's fidelity to his mistress was a supreme
value for which he endured any hardship. Given this context,
the sacredness of Love's pledge was inviolate and could be
utterly trusted (9.3). The soul's failure to be faithful was a serious betrayal (22.9).

Hadewijch also relies on the courtly tradition to speak of a
second quality of the transformed lover—service. The function
of a knight toward his lady was to be her undying servant. He

was ever ready to respond to the call and the needs of his mistress. For Hadewijch, the call to serve Love is the whole point of being involved with God. As a result of the commitment to serve Love, many hardships ensue (18.2), but these difficulties do not dissuade the soul from the tireless performance of good works.

Virtue can never be abandoned as one progresses more deeply into the spiritual life. On the contrary, Hadewijch counsels, "He who begins to make progress / Must see that he does not lose / Zeal for good works" (6.2). The performance of good works gives the lover power and immense profit. As a result, she is able to perform all works "with no sign of effort." Fidelity and passionate commitment to Love have results that defy the imagination. The soul is able to live and suffer with little effort or pain (8.3). This way of living is a fruit of love, a sign of a new self in which earlier experiences have been accepted, embraced, and incorporated into one's total existence. The new self is not turned in on itself, but gracefully faces out toward the neighbor and her or his needs.

> He who wishes to become Love performs excellent
>   works,
> For nothing can make him give way;
> He is unconquered, and equal in strength
> To the task of winning the love of Love,
> Whether he serves the sick or the well,
> The blind, the crippled or the wounded—
> He will accept this as his debt to Love.
>
> To serve strangers, to give to the poor,
> To comfort the sorrowful as best he can,
> To live in the faithful service of God's friends—
> Saints or men on earth—night and day,
> With all his might, beyond possibility—

If he thinks his strength will fail,
Let him trust henceforth in reliance on Love. (8.4–5)

For all her talk about the contours and nuances of passionate love, the bottom line for Hadewijch is faithful service to others. She says that some people think they are successful in love because "[m]ountain and valley burst into bloom." But the ultimate test is not found in the feeling of romantic euphoria but in remaining faithful to a life of virtue on behalf of others. "By works of fidelity it is fully proved / Whether we gain anything in love" (13.5).

Joy and Hope

Hadewijch's experience of Love is riddled with enigma and hardship. Love buffets her with ill treatment and consolation at the same time (31.4). On the one hand, her whole being cries out to devote herself to noble thoughts of Love, for Love enlarges her heart, luring her to give herself completely. But if Hadewijch decides to take any delight or even some brief repose in Love's grace, Love storms at her with new commands, inflicts blows, and casts her into prison (31.1–2). Yet in the midst of this paradox and confusion, Hadewijch maintains a joy, trust, and openness to Love that is difficult to fathom.

For Hadewijch, Love's ways are ineffable, beyond the ken of the human mind (31.3, 7). But this is no reason to give up or become cynical. She simply becomes more motivated to continue on her path of fidelity to Love. She has been captivated by the intense experience of Love and she permits nothing to stand in its way. Her text exudes hope and a deep optimism.

Through Love I can fully conquer
My misery and exile;
I know victory will be mine. (16.4)

Hadewijch counsels her readers to be joyful in all seasons because of Love (30.1). She encourages and exhorts her sisters not to let their grief distress them. "You shall soon blossom," she says, "You shall row through all storms / Until Beloved and loved one shall wholly flow through each other" (4.8). The experience of intimacy with the Beloved is worth any price since its consummation has been promised by a faithful lover. The source of her optimism is Love's promise that can be trusted, her own experience of Love, and Love's inability to withdraw. She says that the soul is to

> ...live in high hope
> Of what his heart has chosen.
> Love will indeed strength him:
> He shall conquer his Beloved;
> For Love can never
> Refuse herself to anyone;
> Rather she gives him what she is willing he possess,
> And more than she herself promised him. (6.2)

No matter what happens in the course of the love affair, the outcome, Hadewijch says, is always joy (6.3).

From this brief excursus into the world and texts of Hadewijch of Brabant, we discover how deeply immersed she was in a mutually passionate love affair with Love. There are other things we could have discussed with profit: the portrait of the human person embedded in the poetry, her nuanced analysis of the madness of love, the way in which she poetically weaves together a tapestry of opposites, her surprising confidence and self–assurance in the truth of what she experienced. Readers are invited to take up her texts in order to probe these and their own questions further.

Hadewijch's talk of intimate love is oriented outward. It is clear that a primary reason for writing is her desire that others know and enjoy in their own way what she has experienced. Her words reach out from every page, inviting and challenging the reader to heed her advice to be open to a passionate love affair with God and with life. She humbly and honestly describes her abandonment to Love:

> To be reduced to nothingness in Love
> Is the most desirable thing I know
> Among all the works I have experience of,
> Although I know it is beyond my reach.

And she cries out to others:

> O soul, creature
> And noble image,
> Risk the adventure!
> Consider your law and your nature—
> Which must always love—
> And love the best good of Love.
> To have fruition of her, defend yourself boldly;
> Thus you will have success.
> And spare no hour,
> But ever keep on to the end
> In love. (36.6)

Conclusion

Hadewijch's use of the courtly love tradition to express her passionate experience of God distances her from the postmodern world, in which women juggle family and boardroom with prayer and spirituality. Few of us see ourselves as knights, although we might identify with the "wounds of love" in her image of a shield covered with dents. But the medieval beguine lifestyle may provoke reflection as we search for intentional

Christian communities beyond the more formal structures of vowed religious life and Sunday worship. She surely addresses our desire to live a more engaged and passionate Christian life.

Her at–times jealous, even vindictive, God might serve to shake up our complacent, and possibly boring images of God. Do we meet a God who encounters us at the deepest level of our being, or are we like ships passing in the blur of a busy life? Hadewijch's God is not someone to take lightly. She and God are serious about their relationship and committed to each other to the death. Emotions run the gamut from profound love and trust to anger, jealousy, doubt and despair. In so many ways, the metaphors of spouse and lover aptly describe their relationship.

Others may be drawn to the sheer artistry of her poetry. Her metaphors and lyric expression remind us that one important aspect of intense love is beauty. Christian spirituality often pays more attention to goodness and truth than to beauty. Hadewijch helps us connect the aesthetic dimensions of nature and humanity with the beauty of God and the spiritual life. Her words also lead us to reflect on romance. Do we see romance only in terms of new, starry–eyed lovers, or can it perdure throughout the long haul of life with God and with each other—the gentle touch, the generous compliment, the surprise gift, the loving gaze? And in her talk of surrender, Hadewijch raises the very thorny question of what this term might possibly mean for both women and men of the twenty–first century. Should one surrender to loved ones, strangers, God, life? Is surrender something we experience at all—and if we do, is it good, destructive, puzzling, or is it simply an arcane remnant from a distant past that needs to be left behind?

In our post–Enlightenment love affair with reason, Hadewijch helps the reader weigh the contributions of love. Her experience and analysis of the relationship of love and reason are honest and realistic. She baptizes neither, and knows instinctively that she must give each its due. We too can reflect on the roles we give to each and whether we are happy with the mix. Reason and common sense can edge out deep feeling—our ability to suffer, rejoice, get angry, weep, and gnash our teeth at our own and the world's sinfulness.

But perhaps Hadewijch's work and the life behind it call us above all to "life" rather than death. Her poetry is a thirteenth–century version of the challenge of Deuteronomy: "I have set before you life and death, blessings and curses. Choose life so that you and your descendants may live, loving the Lord your God, obeying him and holding fast to him; for that means life to you and length of days" (Deut 30:19–20). Hadewijch's love affair with God caused her to live with energy, courage, and intense love. Can we imagine a God who loves us passionately and who, with every fiber of her being, wishes us well, and calls us forth to lives, not of quiet desperation, but of dedicated commitment to work for love and justice in the world? We use expressions like "go the whole nine yards," "give it your all," one–tracker," "leave no holds barred," or "stone unturned." All of which is to wish for each other the sentiment of poet Mary Oliver, who reflects on death:

> When it's over, I don't want to wonder
> If I have made of my life something particular, and
>   real.
> I don't want to find myself sighing and frightened,
> or full of argument.
> I don't want to end up simply having visited this
>   world.[39]

Conclusion

Back to the Present

At the end of our excursion into the nature of passionate love in the mystical writings of Hildegard and Hadewijch, we return to the more mundane terrain of everyday life and spirituality. Does this material speak to us today? Do we find ourselves linked to the long Christian mystical tradition that began with Origen and Augustine, and came to full flowering in the Middle Ages? We have seen many of the ways in which affective expression was embodied in what Bernard McGinn calls vernacular theology, distinguishing it from other medieval forms of theology, namely, the monastic and the scholastic. Vernacular theology has become a constant presence in the history of Christian thought—at times valued and welcomed, at times devalued and marginalized. The strong emotions behind the texts we have examined, communicated to the receptive reader through creative rhetorical strategies, can serve as a needed resource for both contemporary spirituality and theology.

It is my hope that the freshness of expression and the substance of thought in these texts have put a new face on our understanding of passion in the spiritual life. Clarissa Atkinson writes of the medieval affective tradition, "[T]he aim was...to

139

move the heart of the believer. Generally this was accomplished through a personal, passionate attachment to the human man Jesus, and particularly to the aspects of Christ's life which belong to universal human experience: birth and death, Nativity and Passion. Emotions were stirred to wonder and joy, bitter grief and sadness, and tears were actively sought as natural accompaniments to participation in the Christian story."[1]

In our theology, we look to the incarnation as an important foundation for a holistic outlook on the spiritual life that includes both matter and spirit. From the beginning, the Christian community struggled to embrace the full effect of incarnation. If all reality has been made definitively holy by God's taking on flesh in Jesus of Nazareth, then nothing in human life is excluded from the sacred. The experience of passion is no exception. There is no reason *not* to look for and find God in the passionate dimensions of our existence—wherever that passion expresses itself. We are also more aware of the passionate expressions and activities of Jesus himself. While physical sexual activity seems not to have been a part of Jesus' experience, the gospels describe a man who opened himself to others, allowed himself to be led into the fullness of life beyond law and convention, and suffered the inevitable consequences. The gospel demand for radical commitment is the same demand that passion makes in its various forms.[2]

In an article on the power of religious ritual to form and transform the affections, Don Saliers reminds us that "we come to know the deepest and most intimate things through our having and cultivating certain emotions."[3] He cites eighteenth–century New England theologian and preacher, Jonathan Edwards, who reminds us of the importance of the affections:

> Take away all love and hatred, all hope and fear, all anger, zeal and affectionate desire, and the world would be in great measure motionless and dead; there

would be no such things as activity amongst mankind, or any earnest pursuit whatsoever....And as in worldly things worldly affections are very much the spring of men's motion and action; so in religious matters the spring of their actions is very much religious affection....[4]

The hopes and fears of our hearts, our passionate engagements and commitments, reveal more about our intentions and actions, and our present and future identity, than is visible in words or ideas. And the primary location for deep emotions is our everyday life, embedded as it is in the physical and mundane as well as the spiritual and sublime.[5]

Passion fires the heart to love in many ways. In addition to the love of romance, family, and friendship, passionate love drives us to the love of justice for everyone—even our enemies. Moral passion does more than enhance the practice of virtues. It is at the heart of an ethical life, making judgments, propelling us beyond duty and responsibility, endowing action with spontaneity, freedom, and commitment. In the texts we have studied, the reader is struck by these qualities—there is an abandon, a sense of engagement that brooks no obstacles. The fear and paranoia about erotic expression in the spiritual life that characterizes some later Christian attitudes are notably absent.

The reasons for shutting out passion are legion. Fear and cowardice close doors to intensity and commitment. It *is* dangerous to live passionately, and some may mistake fanaticism for true passion and be rightly repulsed by it. But the price of refusing genuine passion is high. It can cost us our lives, condemning us to superficiality, mediocrity, and what Walter Brueggemann calls "under–living."

These texts can also open the door to conversation with those who are passionately committed to faiths other than Christianity. In particular, Hadewijch's conception of Love in her *Poems in Stanzas* can be useful as Christians open themselves to learn about religious faiths beyond Christianity. This potential rests on two factors. First, the foundation of Hadewijch's spirituality is clearly and strongly christological. It is the man Jesus who is at the center of her life. Strong grounding in one's own tradition is the first requirement of fruitful ecumenical and interreligious dialogue. Second, in her *Poems in Stanzas*, Hadewijch speaks of God as Love, personifying God as female. Such a divine name can lead to discussion with a range of mystical traditions, from Jewish Cabbalism to Islamic Sufism.

However, there is one aspect in which the meaning of spiritual passion needs to be quite radically shifted from earlier contexts and meaning. This shift requires that we no longer set up antagonisms between spiritual passion and physical, sexual, erotic expressions of love. While many medieval mystics used human sexual imagery to describe their love affairs with God, they were unable to validate and celebrate human sexual love. They never cease to remind us of the *spiritual* nature of this imagery, and the need for distance between mystical love on the one hand and human, physical sexuality on the other. The point is not to condemn the past because it was different from the present. The literature we have examined was created within a Neoplatonic context that saw flesh and spirit in ways that no longer provide meaning. The world, the physical body, and the passions are portrayed as inimical, yet somehow integral, to the spiritual journey. Though medieval mystics dealt with tensions between matter and spirit in creative and memorable ways, their religious and monastic contexts bequeathed a legacy of antagonism. Their legitimate, beautiful, and still meaningful praise of spiritual passion came at a cost that we are no longer willing to pay—the inability to see the inherent potential for holiness in material and physical expressions of love.

We ask new questions about the relationship between spiritual and physical passion. If experiences of passionate engagement among humans have provided the tradition with a well-spring of language and imagery through which to express passionate encounter with God, we are now able to consider ways in which the religious experience of mystics has the potential to shed light on experiences of passion in human life, and to endow such experiences with value and religious meaning. An important reason to engage in this work is to begin to envision a *mutual* flow—not just from human love to divine love but from divine love to human love. The point is not only to become more open to the possibility of intense engagement with God, but also to celebrate the sacredness and beauty of our passionate encounters with each other.

In contemporary society we are bombarded by explicit sexual images and activity in film, television, song lyrics, clothing, and advertising. One wonders if the traditional religious devaluation of legitimate physical, sexual passion does not contribute to our lack of reverence for sexuality. Would the casual and often promiscuous portrayal of sexuality continue to flourish if we managed to link genuine physical passion with spiritual values and commitments? Can we find ways to allow the erotic language of mystical love that now seems strange and without value to come to our rescue in bodily as well as spiritual ways? Unlike our Christian foremothers in the Middle Ages, we are aware that all of life can be characterized as sexual, inasmuch as everything we think, say, or do, we do as sexual beings. Although sexuality is only one aspect of life, Freud has shown how central it is. We express our sexuality in all aspects of our lives whether we are married, single, vowed to celibacy, gay or straight, young or old.

We can allow the literature we have just examined to precipitate questions about how intense, passionate, physical, and spiritual love can mutually enhance and bestow value on each other. Loving human relationships reveal how we might love God, and loving God can provide light and grace in human relationships. It would impoverish us to allow either form to slip from our consciousness of what the spiritual life entails. The task at hand, then, is to discover connections between passionate attachments in our lives and our religious experience.[6]

I agree with Rosemary Haughton that human sexual relationships are the paradigm or "type" of passion.[7] In its authentic form—that is, when not motivated by selfishness—the human sexual relationship involves a drive to know the other, a drive that stretches out to embrace the whole of living and extends ultimately to God, who is its source. By its very nature, the graced sexual relationship contains the conditions for its own development toward wholeness. It is time for the Christian community to look to sexual love as an important locus and model for our spiritual lives.

I have offered Hildegard and Hadewijch as models for Christians who seek a more intimate and committed relationship with God and the world. Their willingness to become passionately involved with God in Christ made them alive with love. As women of faith, they are anything but boring. Their lives teem with intense participation in divine and human life. They said yes to being in love and accepted the consequences—from joys and satisfactions to dangers and tribulations. They lived courageously and allowed love to assist them in the practice of virtue and in offering a prophetic word to their worlds. By opening themselves to passion, they became different people. At each stage of development, another level of newness broke in upon them, leading them to maturity and integrity of life in imitation of the Lover who chose to lay down his life for them.

We have come full circle and can now respond to the question posed at the beginning. Yes, it is indeed possible to broaden the horizons of our understanding of passion and to live transformed lives as a result. It is possible to allow new insight to calm our fears and remove undue caution about the dangers passion can bring. Yes—to indulge passion in narcissistic and uncontrolled ways is to produce a dissipated and undisciplined life. But to refuse authentic passion is to choose a flat, indifferent, and lukewarm existence. As representatives of the rich and diverse Christian mystical tradition, Hildegard and Hadewijch challenge us—women and men alike—to become fully alive, passionate toward God and others, passionate about becoming saints. Like us, they are both weird and wonderful. When their work is recovered *critically*, it can serve as a catalyst, nudging us to discover new connections with other forms of passionate life—connections unavailable to them in their age.

Hildegard and Hadewijch remind us that we are not alone in our longing for passion in our lives. Echoes of this desire reverberate in time. In the early years of the twentieth century, Spanish existentialist philosopher Miguel de Unamuno wrote:

> Those who say that they believe in God and yet neither love nor fear [God], do not in fact believe in Him, but in those who have taught them that God exists....Those who believe that they believe in God, but without any passion in their heart, without anguish of mind, without uncertainty, without doubt, without an element of despair even in their consolation, believe only in the God–Idea, not in God.[8]

Hildegard and Hadewijch knew intimately a passionate God who freely and generously invited them to share in that divine passion. They responded affirmatively and challenge us to do the same. Openness to the passion of God is guaranteed to call us out of the shallow moral security of obedience to law toward our own deepest humanity. Haughton sees adherence to the law as a crucial preparation, enabling us to distinguish the authentic demand of passion from the fantasies of escapism and self–indulgence. But the law is never enough in itself to satisfy the need of the human spirit for union with God and a love affair with the world.[9]

Passion involves a transformation in which love of others, the desire to heal, to offer comfort and hope, to persevere in suffering, and to offer forgiveness take on a radically new character. When we allow authentic passion to have its way, we can return to love, and life, and service with new verve and feeling. The experience of passion wounds with the fire of love and opens the door to the utter fullness of humanity in God.

Notes

Introduction

1. In the thirteenth century, Thomas Aquinas dealt extensively with the subject of the passions in his treatment of human acts. While we may lament his choice to locate the passions in the sensitive appetite, calling it a "movement of the irrational soul," we can learn from, and applaud, his insight that passion can increase the goodness of an action. According to Thomas, the passions of the soul stand in a twofold relation to the judgment of reason—passions can obscure reason's judgment, but they can also enhance it by way of choice "when a person by the judgment of reason, chooses to be affected by a passion in order to work more promptly with the cooperation of the sensitive appetite. And thus a passion of the soul increases the goodness of an action." *Summa theologiae*, I–II, q. 22, a. 3 and q. 24, a. 3, resp.

2. Bernard McGinn, *The Foundations of Mysticism: Origins to the Fifth Century*, vol 1 of *The Presence of God: A History of Western Christian Mysticism* (New York: Crossroad, 1991), xvii.

3. Thomas F. O'Meara, *Thomas Aquinas Theologian* (Notre Dame, IN: University of Notre Dame Press, 1997), 123. See also Stephen Pope, *The Ethics of Aquinas*, Moral Traditions Series (Washington, DC: Georgetown University Press, 2002).

4. Meredith B. McGuire, "Why Bodies Matter: A Sociological Reflection on Spirituality and Materiality," *Spiritus* 3/1 (Spring 2003): 1–2. See also *Lived Religion in America*, ed. Donald Hall (Princeton, NJ: Princeton University Press, 1997).

5. Walter Principe, "Spirituality, Christian," in *The New Dictionary of Catholic Spirituality*, ed. Michael Downey (Collegeville, MN: The Liturgical Press, 1993). See also Sandra Schneiders, "Spirituality in the Academy," *Theological Studies* 50 (1989): 679–97.

6. John C. Hirsh, "Religious Attitudes and Mystical Language in Medieval Literary Texts: An Essay in Methodology," in *Vox Mystica:*

Essays on Medieval Mysticism in Honor of Professor Valerie M. Lagorio, ed. Anne Clark Bartlett et al. (London: D.S. Brewer, 1995), 16–17.

7. McGinn, *The Foundations of Mysticism*, xvii.

8. Joan Mueller, *Clare of Assisi: The Letters to Agnes* (Collegeville, MN: The Liturgical Press, 2003), 102.

9. See Karl Rahner, "How to Receive a Sacrament and Mean It," *Theology Digest* 19/3 (Autumn 1971): 227–34; William Dych, *Karl Rahner* (London: Geoffrey Chapman, 1992); Declan Marmion, *A Spirituality of Everyday Faith: A Theological Investigation of the Notion of Spirituality in Karl Rahner*, Louvain Theological & Pastoral Monographs, 23 (Louvain: Peeters Press, 1998); Leo O'Donovan, ed., *A World of Grace: An Introduction to the Themes and Foundations of Karl Rahner's Theology* (New York: Seabury Press, 1980); Michael Skelley, *The Liturgy of the World: Karl Rahner's Theology of Worship* (Collegeville, MN: The Liturgical Press, 1991).

10. See Elizabeth A. Dreyer, *Earth Crammed with Heaven: A Spirituality of Everyday Life* (New York/Mahwah, NJ: Paulist Press, 1994); "The Christian in the Workplace" and "Towards A Spirituality of Work," *New Theology Review* 2 (May 1989): 40–65; William John Fitzgerald, *Stories of Coming Home: Finding Spirituality in Our Messy Lives* (New York/Mahwah, NJ: Paulist Press, 1998); Virginia Sullivan Finn, *Pilgrims in This World: A Lay Spirituality* (New York/Mahwah, NJ: Paulist Press, 1990); John C. Haughey, *Converting 9 to 5: Bringing Spirituality to Your Daily Work* (New York: Crossroad, 1994); William E. Diehl, *The Monday Connection* (San Francisco: Harper & Row, 1991); Rosemary Haughton, *Images for Change: The Transformation of Society* (New York/Mahwah, NJ: Paulist Press, 1997); Patrick Henry, *The Ironic Christian's Companion: Finding the Marks of God's Grace in the World* (New York: Riverhead Books, 1999); Samuel Keen, *Hymns to an Unknown God: Awakening the Spirit in Everyday Life* (New York: Bantam Books, 1994); Dolores Lecky, *The Ordinary Way* (New York: Crossroad, 1982); Kathleen Norris, *The Quotidian Mysteries: Laundry, Liturgy, and "Women's Work"* (New York/Mahwah, NJ: Paulist Press, 1998); Parker Palmer, *The Active Life: Wisdom for Work, Creativity, and Caring* (San Francisco: HarperSanFrancisco, 1990); Joan Chittister, *Wisdom Distilled from the Daily: Living the Rule of St. Benedict Today* (San Francisco: Harper & Row, 1991); Lynda Sexson, *Ordinarily Sacred* (Charlottsville and London: University Press of Virginia, 1992); William Reiser, *To Hear God's Word*,

Listen to the Word: The Liberation of Spirituality (New York/Mahwah, NJ: Paulist Press, 1997).

11. For example, see Jeffrey J. Kripal, *Roads of Excess, Palaces of Wisdom: Eroticism & Reflexivity in the Study of Mysticism* (Chicago: University of Chicago Press, 2001), 1–33, 306–8.

12. Andrew Weeks, *German Mysticism from Hildegard of Bingen to Ludwig Wittgenstein: A Literary and Intellectual History*, SUNY Series in Western Esoteric Traditions, ed. David Appelbaum (Albany, NY: SUNY, 1993), 9.

13. Ibid.

14. What follows is a revised and updated version of my Madeleva Lecture, *Passionate Women: Two Medieval Mystics* (New York/Mahwah, NJ: Paulist Press, 1989), now out of print. With permission of St. Mary's College, Notre Dame, IN.

15. In an op–ed essay in *The New York Times* entitled "Believe It, Or Not," Nicholas D. Kristof voices concern for what he sees as the growing dominance of affective, "mystical" faith and the decline of the great intellectual traditions of both Catholic and Protestant churches in America. A careful reading of mystical texts challenges his linkage of the term *mysticism* with the intellectually soft and emotionally naïve. As we will discover, the great mystics succeed in holding together the affective and the intellectual aspects of the spiritual life in creative and convincing ways. *The New York Times* (August 15, 2003), A29.

1. Medieval Women Mystics: Weird or Wonderful?

1. Barbara Newman, *From Virile Woman to WomanChrist: Studies in Medieval Religion and Literature* (Philadelphia: University of Pennsylvania Press, 1995), 1.

2. Carole Slade, *St. Teresa of Avila: Author of a Heroic Life* (Berkeley: University of California Press, 1995), 6–7.

3. Gerda Lerner, *The Creation of Feminist Consciousness* (New York: Oxford University Press, 1993), vii–viii.

4. Susan Mosher Stuard, "A New Dimension?: North American Scholars Contribute Their Perspective," in *Women in Medieval History & Historiography*, ed. Susan Mosher Stuard (Philadelphia: University of Pennsylvania Press, 1987), 94.

5. Grace Janzen, "Disrupting the Sacred: Religion and Gender in the City," in *Mysticism & Social Transformation*, ed. Janet K. Ruffing (Syracuse, NY: Syracuse University Press, 2001), 29.

6. Luce Irigaray, *Sexes and Genealogies*, trans. Gillian C. Gill (New York: Columbia University Press, 1993), 75. Cited in Jantzen, "Disrupting the Sacred," 29.

7. Jantzen, "Disrupting the Sacred," 44.

8. Katharina Wilson, ed., *Medieval Women Writers* (Athens: University of Georgia Press, 1984), viii.

9. Many publishing houses have volumes of excerpts from the works of individual mystics. See especially the series by Paulist Press, The Classics of Western Spirituality.

10. *Acts of Justine and Companions; Martyrs of Lyons and Vienne; Acts of the Scillitan Martyrs; Martyrdom of Sts. Carpus, Papylus, and Agathonice; Passion of Sts. Perpetua and Felicitas; Martyrdom of Potamiaena and Basilides; Martyrdom of Pionius the Presbyter and His Companions; Martyrdom of Agape, Irene, Chione, and Companions; Martyrdom of St. Crispina.* See Herbert Mursillo, *Acts of the Christian Martyrs*, Oxford Early Christian Texts (Oxford: Clarendon, 1972).

11. This text can be found in Elizabeth Avilda Petroff, ed., *Medieval Women's Visionary Literature* (Oxford: Oxford University Press, 1986), 70–77; and Shawn Madigan, ed., *Mystics, Visionaries and Prophets: A Historical Anthology of Women's Spiritual Writings* (Minneapolis: Fortress Press, 1998), 9–25.

12. Excerpts of this text can be found in Madigan, 74–90.

13. See Wilson, *Medieval Women Writers*, 30–63; and Petroff, *Medieval Women's Visionary Literature*, 124–35.

14. See Mary Duydam, "Beguine Textuality: Sacred Performances," in *Performance and Transformation: New Approaches to Late Medieval Spirituality* (New York: St. Martin's Press, 1999), 176–79; and John Dagenais, *The Ethics of Reading in a Manuscript Culture: Glossing the Libro de Buen Amor* (Princeton, NJ: Princeton University Press, 1994).

15. Hildegard of Bingen, *Scivias* (New York/Mahwah, NJ: Paulist Press, 1990), 536.

16. See *Gendered Voices: Medieval Saints and Their Interpreters*, ed. Catherine M. Mooney (Philadelphia: University of Pennsylvania Press, 1999).

17. Caroline Walker Bynum, *Holy Feast, Holy Fast* (Berkeley: University of California Press, 1987), 29.

18. John Anson, "The Female Transvestite in Early Monasticism: The Origin and Development of a Motif," *Viator* 5 (1974): 1–32.

19. Early forms of Benedictine life (600–1200) did not follow this pattern. For example, Boniface, Leoba, Walburga, and Hilda were active missionaries, involved in education, politics, and ecclesiastical debates. As we will see in chapter 4, beguine communities in the thirteenth century also had extensive contact with the world.

20. Henry of Ghent, *Summae Quaestionum Ordinarium*, vol. 1 (Paris: Badius Ascensius, 1520; reprint, St. Bonaventure, NY: The Franciscan Institute, 1953), art. XI, quaest. 11, ff. 77v–78r. Cited in Bernard McGinn, ed., *Meister Eckhart and the Beguine Mystics: Hadewijch of Brabant, Mechthild of Magdeburg, and Marguerite Porete* (New York: Continuum, 1994), 1.

21. Psychological and medical analyses of this material range from honest engagement to dismissal. A recent example of the former is *Saints and Madmen: Psychiatry Opens Its Doors to Religion*, Russell Shorto (New York: Henry Holt, 1999).

22. Carol Lee Flinders, *At the Root of Our Longing: Reconciling a Spiritual Hunger and a Feminist Thirst* (San Francisco: HarperSan Francisco, 1998), 175–77.

23. Bynum, *Holy Feast*, 299.

24. Ibid.

25. Ibid., 114.

26. Raymond of Capua, *The Life of Catherine of Siena*, trans. Conleth Kearns (Wilmington, DE: Michael Glazier, 1980), 155–56.

27. This letter does not appear in the first two volumes of Suzanne Noffke's translations of Catherine's letters. *The Letters of Catherine of Siena*, Medieval and Renaissance Texts and Studies, vols. 202 and 203 (Tempe: Arizona Center for Medieval and Renaissance Studies, 2002, 2003). This letter in Italian can be found as Letter 86 in *Le lettere di S. Caterina da Siena*, ed. Piero Misciattelli (Siena: Giuntini e Bentivoglio, 1913–21), vol. 2, pp. 81–82.

28. Bynum, *Holy Feast*, 175.

29. This story can be found in St. Bonaventure's *Life of Francis*, Classics of Western Spirituality (New York/Mahwah, NJ: Paulist Press, 1978), 188–89.

30. Bynum, *Holy Feast*, 199.

31. Angela of Foligno, *The Book of the Blessed Angela of Foligno*, trans. Paul Lachance (New York/Mahwah, NJ: Paulist Press, 1993), 196–97.

32. Bynum, *Holy Feast*, 114.

33. Ibid., 207.

34. Ibid., 209.

35. See *Women & Power in the Middle Ages*, eds. Mary Erler and Maryanne Kowaleski (Athens: University of Georgia Press, 1988); *Power, Gender and Christian Mysticism*, by Grace M. Jantzen (Cambridge: Cambridge University Press, 1995); and *Power of the Weak: Studies on Medieval Women*, eds. Jennifer Carpenter and Sally–Beth MacLean (Urbana and Chicago: University of Illinois Press, 1995).

36. It is important to distinguish between the spirituality found in works written by the women themselves and in works authored by male colleagues. See Michael Goodich, "The Contours of Female Piety in Later Medieval Hagiography," *Church History* 50/1 (March 1981): 20–32.

37. See Joan M. Ferrante, "The Education of Women in the Middle Ages in Theory, Fact, and Fantasy," in *Beyond Their Sex: Learned Women of the European Past*, ed. Patricia H. Labalme (New York: New York University Press, 1980), 9–42.

38. Gertrude the Great of Helfta, *Spiritual Exercises* (Kalamazoo, MI: Cistercian Publications, 1989).

39. Julian of Norwich, *Showings* (New York/Mahwah, NJ: Paulist Press, 1978).

40. See Teresa of Avila, *The Way of Perfection*, prologue, 3; ch. 4.13–16 in *The Collected Works of St. Teresa of Avila*, vol. 2, trans. Kieran Kavanaugh and Otilio Rodriguez (Washington, DC: ICS Publications, 1980), 42, 57–58; *The Interior Castle*, VI.1.8–9; VI.3.8; VI.6.1–2; VI.8.9; VI.9.13 (New York/Mahwah, NJ: Paulist Press, 1979), 111–13, 122, 137–38, 155, 160; *The Book of Her Life*, Ch. XXIII and XXX in *The Collected Works of St. Teresa of Avila*, vol. 1, trans. Kieran Kavanaugh and Otilio Rodriguez (Washington, DC: ICS Publications, 1976), 152, 194.

41. Peter Dronke, *Medieval Women Writers* (Cambridge: Cambridge University Press, 1984), 201.

42. See *Teresa of Avila and the Rhetoric of Feminity*, by Alison Weber (Princeton, NJ: Princeton University Press, 1990).

43. Marguerite Porete, *The Mirror of Simple Souls* (New York/Mahwah, NJ: Paulist Press, 1993).

44. See Barbara Newman, "Possessed by the Spirit: Devout Women, Demoniacs, and the Apostolic Life in the Thirteenth Century," *Speculum* 73 (1998): 734–41.

45. Julian of Norwich, *Showings*, 183, 186.

46. Caroline Walker Bynum, *Jesus As Mother* (Berkeley: University of California Press, 1982), 17.

47. For a thorough study of the Eucharist in the Middle Ages, see Miri Rubin, *Corpus Christi: The Eucharist in Late Medieval Culture* (Cambridge: Cambridge University Press, 1991).

48. Bynum, *Jesus As Mother*, 191, 215.

49. Gertrude of Helfta, *Spiritual Exercises*, 59.

50. Ibid., 67.

51. Hadewijch: *The Complete Works* (New York/Mahwah, NJ: Paulist Press, 1980), 268.

52. Ibid., 269.

53. Julian of Norwich, *Showings*, 181.

54. Ibid., 183, 186.

55. Ibid., 246.

56. Ibid., 212.

57. Ibid., 213.

58. Teresa of Avila, *The Book of Her Life*, ch. IX.3, in *The Collected Works of St. Teresa of Avila*, 71.

59. Ibid., ch. XXII.1, 144.

60. Hadewijch, *The Complete Works*, 344.

61. Julian of Norwich, *Showings*, 216.

62. Marguerite Porete, *Mirror of Simple Souls*. Cited by Peter Dronke, *Women Writers of the Middle Ages* (Cambridge: Cambridge University Press, 1984), 221–22.

63. Julian of Norwich, *Showings*, 216.

64. Ibid., 230–31.

65. Teresa of Avila, *Interior Castle*, IV.2.12.

66. Julian of Norwich, *Showings*, 289.

67. Rosemary Haughton, *On Trying to Be Human* (Springfield, IL: Templegate, 1966), 93.

68. Hadewijch, Letter 18, *Complete Works*, 86.

69. Hadewijch, *Complete Works*, 352.

70. *The Prayers of Catherine of Siena*, ed. Suzanne Noffke (New York/Mahwah, NJ: Paulist Press, 1983), 58.

71. Ibid., 54.

72. Hadewijch, *Complete Works*, 135.

73. Hildegard of Bingen, *Vita*, cited in Peter Dronke, *Medieval Women Writers*, 145.

74. Julian of Norwich, *Showings*, 229.

2. Passion in the Christian Tradition

1. Simon Tugwell, *Prayer in Practice* (Springfield, IL: Templegate, 1974), 50–51.

2. I rely here on the *Oxford English Dictionary*, s.v. "passion." *Webster's Dictionary* defines passion as (a) suffering or agony; (b) compelling emotion such as enthusiasm, strong love, or desire. Synonyms include ardor, attachment, devotion, pathos, rapture, vehemence, zeal.

3. See Elizabeth A. Dreyer, "Love," in *The New Dictionary of Catholic Spirituality*, ed. Michael Downey (Collegeville, MN: The Liturgical Press, 1993), 613: "Broadly stated, love is an affective disposition toward another person [or thing] arising from qualities perceived as attractive, from instincts of natural relationship, or from sympathy, and resulting in concern for the welfare of the object and usually also delight in her/his/its presence and desire for the beloved's acceptance and approval. From a religious perspective, love is considered to be preeminently God's benevolent love."

4. For an excellent treatment of these themes see Bernard McGinn, *The Foundations of Mysticism: Origins to the Fifth Century*, vol. 1 of *The Presence of God: A History of Christian Mysticism* (New York: Crossroad, 1991), 84–130.

5. Plotinus, *Enneads* I.8.

6. A. H. Armstrong, "The Ancient and Continuing Pieties of the Greek World," in *Classical Mediterranean Spirituality*, ed. A. H. Armstrong, World Spirituality Series, vol. 15 (New York: Crossroad, 1986), 70.

7. Ibid., 85.

8. Ibid.

9. Ibid.

10. Plato discusses the various aspects of love in the *Phaedrus*. The story of the chariot can be found in *The Dialogues of Plato*, trans. B. Jowett, vol. 1 (New York: Random House, 1920), 250–53.

11. Aristotle, *Nichomachean Ethics*, trans. David Ross (Oxford: Oxford University Press, 1998), Book VIII, chapters 3 and 13.

12. Armstrong, 86. In the *City of God*, Augustine explains the teaching of the Stoics on passion in light of the Christian gospel (14.8). Martha Nussbaum retrieves this tradition in what she calls a "Neo–Stoic" view of the role of the affections in the moral life in her *Upheavals of Thought: The Intelligence of Emotions* (Cambridge: Cambridge University Press, 2001).

13. See Bernard McGinn, *The Foundations of Mysticism*, 131–185.

14. Philo Judaeus, *On Creation*, ed. F. H. Colson (London: Heinemann, 1929), 227. Cited in R. Howard Bloch, *Medieval Misogyny and the Invention of Western Romantic Love* (Chicago: University of Chicago Press, 1991), 29.

15. Michael Casey, "Apatheia," *The New Dictionary of Christian Spirituality*, ed. Michael Downey (Collegeville, MN: The Liturgical Press, 1993), 50–51.

16. Cited in Bernard McGinn, *The Foundations of Mysticism*, 151–52.

17. Many seekers from affluent countries have turned to Buddhist disciplines, especially the practice of nonattachment, which is analogous to what we have described as *apatheia*.

18. Bernard McGinn, "The Language of Inner Experience in Christian Mysticism," *Spiritus* 1/2 (Fall 2001): 157.

19. *In Canticum Canticorum*, Hom 1 (ed. Langerbeck, 27.5–15; trans., 49). Cited in Bernard McGinn, "The Language of Inner Experience in Christian Mysticism," 157.

20. Bernard of Clairvaux, Sermon 20.III.4, *On the Song of Songs*, vol. I (Kalamazoo, MI: Cisterican Publications, 1971), 150.

21. For recent analyses of the spiritual senses, see Karl Rahner, *Theological Investigations*, vol. 16 (New York: Seabury, 1979), 104–34; Hans Urs von Balthasar, *The Glory of the Lord: A Theological Aesthetics*, vol. I: *Seeing the Form* (San Francisco–New York: Ignatius–Crossroad, 1982), 365–80; Stephen Fields, "Balthasar and Rahner on the Spiritual Senses," *Theological Studies* 57 (1996): 224–41; Bernard McGinn, "The Language of Inner Experience in Christian Mysticism," *Spiritus* 1/2

(Fall 2001): 156–71; Don Saliers, "Sound Spirituality: On the Formative Expressive Power of Music for Christian Spirituality," *Christian Spirituality Bulletin* 8/1 (Spring/Summer, 2000): 1–5; Sarah Coakley, *Powers and Submissions: Spirituality, Philosophy and Gender* (Oxford: Blackwell, 2002), 130–52.

22. Origen, *Commentary on the Song of Songs*, Prologue. Classics of Western Spirituality (New York/Mahwah, NJ: Paulist Press, 1979), 223.

23. See Olivier Clement, *The Roots of Christian Mysticism: Texts from the Patristic Era with Commentary* (New York: New City Press, 1993).

24. Origen, *Commentary on the Song of Songs*, 217–18.

25. Ibid., 223.

26. This translation of the Prologue to Origen's *Commentary on the Song of Songs* is by R. P. Lawson, *Origen: An Exhortation to Martyrdom. Prayer and Selected Works*, Ancient Christian Writers, 26 (Westminster, MD: Newman, 1957), 34–35. Cited in Bernard McGinn, *The Foundations of Mysticism: Origins to the Fifth Century*, 119–20.

27. For an excellent treatment of these themes, see Peter Brown, *The Body and Society: Men, Women, and Sexual Renunciation in Early Christianity* (New York: Columbia University Press, 1988).

28. Gregory of Nyssa, *Life of Moses*, trans. Abraham J. Malherbe and Everett Ferguson, Classics of Western Spirituality (New York, Ramsey and Toronto: Paulist Press, 1978), 56; *Sermon on the Six Beatitudes*, trans. Hilda Graef, Ancient Christian Writers (Westminster, MD: Newman, 1954), 143–46.

29. Contemporary interest in the recovery of affectivity is growing. In the areas of theology and theological method, one can cite Karl Rahner's theological corpus in which he speaks of ultimate happiness as acceptance of Mystery in love, and Bernard Lonergan's analysis of feelings as the cause of our response to value. For further development of the role of the affections in Lonergan's thought, see Robert Doran, *Theological Foundations: Theology and Culture* and *Theological Foundations: Intentionality and Psyche*, Marquette Studies in Theology, 8–9 (Milwaukee: Marquette University Press, 1995). One can also identify the women's movement as an important force behind recent interest in affectivity. Recovery of the place and dignity of women has meant the recovery of body and feeling with which women have been culturally identified. See also Frances Wilks, *Intelligent Emotion: How to*

Succeed Through Transforming Your Feelings (Burlington, MA: William Heinemann, 1999); Daniel Goleman, *Emotional Intelligence* (New York: Bantam Books, 1997); Daniel Goleman et al., *Primal Leadership: Realizing the Power of Emotional Intelligence* (Cambridge, MA: Harvard Business School Press, 2002).

30. In addition to Martha Nussbaum (n. 12 above), the role of the affections in moral theology has been addressed by Daniel Maguire, who criticizes what he calls the "intellectualistic fallacy" that denies the role of the affections in practical moral reasoning. He notes in particular that such an approach "leaves untouched the mystical and contemplative dimensions of moral consciousness," "*Ratio Practica* and the Intellectualistic Fallacy," *Journal of Religious Ethics* 10 (1982): 22–39. Criticism of Nussbaum from Roman Catholic perspectives include L. Gregory Jones, "The Love Which *Love's Knowledge* Knows Not: Nussbaums' Evasion of Christianity," *The Thomist* 56 (1992): 323–37, and Carlo Leget, "Martha Nussbaum and Thomas Aquinas on the Emotions," *Theological Studies* 64/3 (September 2003): 558–81.

31. In his three volume work, *The Nature of Love*, Irving Singer expresses this sentiment: "[I]n the last sixty years or so the analysis of love has been neglected more than almost any other subject in philosophy." Vol. 1, *Plato to Luther* (Chicago: University of Chicago Press, 1984 [1966]), xi.

32. This tide is gradually changing. See Allan Bloom, *Shakespeare on Love and Friendship* (Chicago: University of Chicago Press, 2000); David B. Burrell, *Friendship and Ways to Truth* (Notre Dame, IN: University of Notre Dame Press, 2000); Diogenes Allen, *Love, Christian Romance, Marriage, Friendship* (Cambridge, MA: Cowley Publications, 1987); Daniel Berrigan, *Sorrow Built a Bridge: Friendship and Aids* (Minneapolis, MN: Fortress Press, 1989); Lawrence A. Blum, *Friendship, Altruism and Morality* (Boston: Routledge & Kegan Paul, 1980); John W. Crossin, *Friendship: The Key to Spiritual Growth* (New York/Mahwah, NJ: Paulist Press, 1997); Mary Hunt, *Fierce Tenderness: Toward a Feminist Theology of Friendship* (San Francisco: Harper & Row, 1989); Alan Jones, *Exploring Spiritual Direction. An Essay on Christian Friendship* (New York: Seabury Press, 1982); Gilbert C. Meilander, *Friendship: A Study in Theological Ethics* (Notre Dame, IN: University of Notre Dame Press, 1981); Martin Marty, *Friendship* (Allen, TX: Tabor Publishing, 1980); Leroy S. Rouner, ed., *The Changing Face of Friendship* (Notre Dame, IN:

University of Notre Dame Press, 1994); Paul Waddell, *Friendship and the Moral Life* (Notre Dame, IN: University of Notre Dame Press, 1989).

33. Exceptions include the *Dictionnaire de spiritualité*, which devotes eighteen columns to the subject under the heading, "Passions et vie spirituelle."

34. Gaylin and Pearson, eds., *Passionate Attachments: Thinking About Love* (New York: Macmillan Free Press, 1988), vii.

35. Irving Singer, *The Nature of Love*, vol. 1, *Plato to Luther*, 29.

36. Ibid. See also vol. 2, *Courtly and Romantic* (1984); vol. 3, *The Modern World* (1987).

37. I am grateful to Dr. Peter Mohrer for insight about the significance and role of love in Freud and in psychoanalytic practice.

38. See W. Gaylin and E. Person, eds., *Passionate Attachments*, ix–xii.

39. Roxana Robinson, "The Big Chill," *New York Times Book Review* (January 7, 2001): 31.

40. Ibid.

41. Ibid. J. Elkins expresses similar sentiments for the field of art history in "The Ivory Tower of Tearlessness," *The Chronicle of Higher Education* (November 9, 2001).

42. Ibid. Robinson compares Jane Smiley's *A Thousand Acres* with Shakespeare's *King Lear*, from whose plot it draws. She acknowledges the brilliance of Smiley's work, but comments on the difference in emotional dynamics. She thinks Smiley's novel lacks much of the humanity that makes Lear so powerful. Lear reveals himself as a humble and passionately devoted father. Smiley's father turns out to be an arrogant tyrant and a ruthless and incestuous child molester. Smiley's world is "illuminated not by sympathy, but by the arctic dazzle of her intelligence."

43. A single example of the many exceptions is the work of Toni Morrison. In a review of Morrison's novel, *Love* (Knopf, 2003), Laura Miller notes how Morrison portrays emotion—it is as much affliction and delusion as joy. In settings marred by the effects of racism, the extreme workings of passion are often indistinguishable from ordinary heartlessness. The core of another novel, *Beloved*, "occupies an emotional terrain where reason doesn't operate or apply." *New York Times Book Review* (November 2, 2003): 10.

44. Robinson lists as examples the work of Richard Ford, Cormac McCarthy, Don DeLillo, Martin Amis, Paul Auster, David Gates, and Robert Stone. Women who follow this mold include Joyce Carol Oates, A.M. Homes, Kathryn Harison, and Lorrie Moore.

45. Scott McLemee, "Getting Emotional," *The Chronicle of Higher Education* (February 21, 2003).

46. For example, *Anger: The Struggle for Emotional Control in America's History*, by Carol Zisowitz Stearns and Peter N. Stearns (Chicago: University of Chicago Press, 1986); *Restraining Rage: The Ideology of Anger Control in Classical Antiquity*, by William V. Harris (Cambridge, MA: Harvard University Press, 2001); *The Vehement Passions*, by Philip Fisher (Princeton, NJ: Princeton University Press, 2002).

47. Examples include *Scenes of Shame: Psychoanalysis, Shame and Writing*, eds. Joseph Adamson and Hilary Clark (Albany: SUNY, 1998); *Shame: Interpersonal Behavior, Psychopathology, and Culture*, by Paul Gilbert and Bernice Andrews (Oxford: Oxford University Press, 1998); *Surprised by Shame: Dostoevsky's Liars and Narrative Exposure*, by Deborah A. Martinsen (Columbus: Ohio State University Press, 2003); *Shame and Its Sisters: A Silvan Tomkins Reader*, eds. Eve Kosojsky Sedgwick and Adam Frank (Atlanta: Duke University Press, 1995); *Shame: Theory, Therapy, Theology* by Stephen Pattison (Cambridge: Cambridge University Press, 2000).

48. See Arlie Russell Hochschild, *The Managed Heart: Commercialization of Human Feeling* (Berkeley: University of California Press, 1983).

49. For a portrait of this type of rugged individualism, see Jane Tompkins' *West of Everything* (Oxford and New York: Oxford University Press, 1992).

50. See Candace B. Pert, *Molecules of Emotion: The Science Behind Mind–Body Medicine* (New York: Simon & Schuster, 1999); Joseph Ledoux, *The Emotional Brain: The Mysterious Underpinnings of Emotional Life* (New York: Simon & Schuster, 1998); Antonio Damasio, *Looking for Spinoza: Joy, Sorrow and the Feeling Brain* (New York: Harcourt, 2003).

51. Bernard McGinn, "Love, Knowledge and *Unio Mystica* in the Western Christian Tradition," in *Mystical Union in Judaism, Christianity, and Islam: An Ecumenical Dialogue* eds. Moshe Idel and Bernard McGinn (New York: Continuum, 1996), 59–86; Bernard McGinn, "The Language of Love in Jewish and Christian Mysticism," in *Mysticism and*

Language, ed. Steven Katz (London: Oxford University Press, 1990); E. Ann Matter, *The Voice of My Beloved: The Song of Songs in Western Medieval Christianity* (Philadelphia: University of Pennsylvania Press, 1990). See also Denys Turner, *Eros and Allegory: Medieval Exegesis of the Song of Songs* (Kalamazoo, MI: Cistercian Publications, 1995); Ann Astell, *The Song of Songs in the Middle Ages* (Ithaca, NY: Cornell University Press, 1990); Michael Fox, *The Song of Songs and the Ancient Egyptian Love Songs* (Madison: University of Wisconsin Press, 1985).

52. Martha Nussbaum, *Poetic Justice: The Literary Imagination and Public Life* (Boston: Beacon Press, 1997), especially chapter 3, "Rational Emotions"; and *The Therapy of Desire* (Princeton: Princeton University Press, 1996); Rita Nakashima Brock, *Journeys by Heart: A Christology of Erotic Power* (New York: Crossroads, 1988); William C. Spohn, "Passions and Principles," *Theological Studies* 52 (March 1991): 69–87 and "The Reasoning Heart: An American Approach to Discernment," *Theological Studies* 44 (March 1983): 30–52. See also Paul Avis, *Eros and the Sacred* (London: SPCK, 1989); Paula Cooey et al. *Embodied Love: Sensuality and Relationship As Feminist Values* (San Francisco: Harper and Row, 1987); Carter Heyward, *Touching Our Strength: The Erotic Power and the Love of God* (San Francisco: Harper and Row, 1989); Blair Reynolds with Patricia Heinicke, Jr. *The Naked Being of God: Making Sense of Love Mysticism* (Lanham, MD: University Press of America, 2000); Catherine Osborne, *Eros Unveiled: Plato and the God of Love* (Oxford: Oxford University Press, 1995). A useful bibliographical tool is John Corrigan, Eric Cramp and John Kloos, eds., *Emotion and Religion: A Critical Assessment and Annotated Bibliography* (Westport, CT: Greenwood Press, 2000).

53. Don E. Saliers, *The Soul in Paraphrase: Prayer and the Religious Affections* (New York: Crossroad, 1980).

54. See *The Song of Songs: A New Translation and Interpretation*, by Marcia Falk (San Francisco: HarperSanFrancisco, 1990); Ariel and Chana Bloch, *The Song of Songs: A New Translation* (Berkeley: University of California Press, 1998); Diane Bergant, *The Song of Songs* (Collegeville, MN: The Liturgical Press, 2001); Roland Murphy *The Song of Songs: A Commentary on the Book of Canticles or The Song of Songs*, ed. S. Dean McBride, Jr. (Minneapolis: Fortress Press, 1990).

55. Bernard McGinn, "Love, Knowledge and *Unio Mystica*," 84, 64.

56. For a concise summary of this Cartesian framework, see the Introduction in *Gender/Body/Knowledge: Feminist Reconstructions of Being and Knowing*, eds. Alison M. Jaggar and Susan R. Bordo (New Brunswick, NJ: Rutgers University Press, 1989), 3. See also Sarah Coakley, *Powers and Submissions*, 75–78.

57. Jaggar and Bordo, *Gender/Body/Knowledge*, 163–65.

58. Writing from an Anglican perspective, Mark McIntosh offers a more integral view of theology in *Mysteries of Faith*, The New Church's Teaching Series, 8 (Boston: Cowley Publications, 2000).

59. Bernard McGinn, *The Flowering of Mysticism: Men and Women in the New Mysticism—1200–1350*, vol. 3 of *The Presence of God: A History of Western Christian Mysticism* (New York: Crossroad Herder, 1998), 20–21.

60. Ibid., 25. In "Bloody Bodies: Gender, Religion, and the State in Nazi Germany," Ulrike Wiethaus comments, "The conflation of hysteria and female mysticism became revived in contemporary French feminist theory, yet with a twist. Hysterical manifestations once deemed pathological have been recast as somatized discourse of resistance and protest beyond phallocentric regimes of truth." In *Studies in Spirituality* 12 (2002): 97, n. 25.

61. Mary Warnock, "Religious Imagination," in *Religious Imagination*, ed. James P. Mackey (Edinburgh: Edinburgh University Press, 1986), 142.

62. See David G. Hunter, "Dualism," in *The New Dictionary of Christian Spirituality*, ed. Michael Downey (Collegeville, MN: The Liturgical Press, 1993), 298–99.

63. Bernard Lonergan, *Method in Theology*, 130–32; 267–93.

64. Michael Buckley, "The Rise of Atheism and the Religious Epoche," in *Proceedings of the Catholic Theological Society of America* 47 (June 11–14, 1992): 69–83.

65. See Rosemary Haughton, *On Trying to Be Human* (Springfield, IL: Templegate, 1966), 93, 104, 108.

66. Milton Viederman citing student dissertation by R. Michels. In "The Nature of Passionate Love," in *Passionate Attachments*, ix–xii.

67. Ibid., 1–4. Viederman distinguishes between passionate and affectionate love. Passionate love occurs in the early stages of a love relationship and is followed by a less intense affectionate love. He also cites Otto Kernberg, who chooses to maintain the term *passion* in both

cases, distinguishing between passion as an early stage of a love relationship and passion as the cement of a more enduring one. The mystics clearly fit into this latter schema in which passionate encounter
with God grows and perdures throughout a lifetime of mutually faithful love.

68. See Irving Singer, *The Nature of Love*, vol. 2, *Courtly and Romantic*, 32.

69. Catherine Mowry LaCugna, *God for Us: The Trinity and Christian Life* (San Francisco: HarperCollins, 1993), 1.

70. Rosemary Haughton, *The Passionate God* (New York/Mahwah, NJ: Paulist Press, 1981).

71. Haughton, *On Trying to Be Human*, 93.

72. Ibid., 106.

73. Haughton, *The Passionate God*, 9.

74. Ibid., 18.

75. Questions about the viability of the metaphysical category
of being, or for that matter of metaphysics in general, are being discussed widely in both philosophical and theological quarters. One
theologian who also advocates a move from a metaphysics of substance to a metaphysics of relational love is Catherine Mowry
LaCugna, *God for Us*. See also Elizabeth T. Groppe, "Catherine Mowry
LaCugna's Contribution to Trinitarian Theology," *Theological Studies*
63/4 (December 2002): 730–63, especially pp. 747–53.

76. Haughton, *The Passionate God*, 21.

77. Examples of different communitarian concepts of the Trinity
have been worked out by Catherine Mowry LaCugna, *God for Us*; and,
from a process theology perspective, Joseph Bracken, *The Triune
Symbol: Persons, Process, and Community* (Lanham, MD: University Press
of America, 1985); "The Holy Trinity as a Community of Divine
Persons," *Heythrop Journal* 15 (1974): 166–82; and "The Trinity as
Interpersonal Process," *Ecumenical Trends* 13 (1984): 97–99.

78. Haughton, *The Passionate God*, 27.

79. Ibid., 26.

80. Ibid., 7.

81. Ibid., 6.

82. Ibid.

83. There are a growing number of books that seek to integrate
sexuality and the Christian life. Among these are Joan Timmerman,

The Mardi Gras Syndrome: Rethinking Christian Sexuality (New York: Crossroad, 1984) and *Sexuality and Spiritual Growth* (New York: Crossroad, 1992); James B. Nelson and Sandra P. Longfellow, eds., *Sexuality and the Sacred: Sources for Theological Reflection* (Louisville: Westminster/John Knox,1994); Evelyn and James Whitehead, *Sexuality and Spiritual Growth* (New York: Crossroad, 1992).

84. Milton Viederman, "The Nature of Passionate Love," 6.

85. For two different treatments of tradition, see Jaroslav Pelikan, *The Vindication of Tradition* (New Haven: Yale University Press, 1986) and John E. Thiel, *Senses of Tradition: Continuity and Development in Catholic Faith* (Oxford: Oxford University Press, 2000).

86. Sayings and stories of wisdom appear throughout the Hebrew scriptures, for example in the prophetic books of Isaiah and Amos. But books that are specifically designated "wisdom" include Proverbs, Job, Ecclesiastes (Qoheleth), Ecclesiasticus (Sirach), the Wisdom of Solomon, the Song of Songs, and certain Psalms (1, 19:8–15, 37, 49, 73, 111, 119).

87. Lawrence Boadt, *Reading the Old Testament: An Introduction* (New York/Mahwah, NJ: Paulist Press, 1984), 479, 491.

88. Elizabeth A. Johnson, *She Who Is: The Mystery of God in Feminist Theological Discourse* (New York: Crossroad, 1992), 86–87, 91.

89. Elisabeth Schüssler Fiorenza, *In Memory of Her: A Feminist Theological Reconstruction of Christian Origins* (New York: Crossroad, 1983), 133.

90. Ibid., 134.

91. Johnson, *She Who Is*, 87.

92. Ibid., 97.

93. Ibid., 91–92.

94. Recent work on the Song of Songs is abundant. See note 54 above.

95. See T. J. Miik, "Babylonian Parallels to the Song of Songs," *Journal of Biblical Literature* 43 (1924): 245–52; and Michael V. Fox, *The Song of Songs & Ancient Egyptian Love Songs* (Madison: University of Wisconsin Press, 1985).

96. William E. Phipps suggests that the editor contributed little to the content and organization of the poem: "Like stringing a necklace, he [editor] loosely put together folk lyrics of varying lengths which added different facets of beauty to the unifying theme." "The

Plight of the Song of Songs," *Journal of the American Academy of Religion* 42 (March 1974): 82. Marcia Falk also suggests that the Song was probably not a unified work in its earliest stages. *The Song of Songs*, xiii.

97. Marvin H. Pope opts for a cultic interpretation. "[T]he cultic interpretation . . . is best able to account for the erotic imagery. Sexuality is a basic human interest and the affirmation that 'God is Love' includes all meanings of both words." *Song of Songs*, Anchor Bible (New York: Doubleday, 1977), 17. "Biblical Interpretation and the Construction of Christian Sexualities" is the theme of the June 2000 (vol. 69/2) issue of *Church History*, which contains articles by Elizabeth A. Clark, David G. Hunter, Shawn M. Krahmer, Stephen D. Moore, Irven M. Resnick, and Belden C. Lane.

98. Origen, *Commentary on the Song of Songs and Homilies* 1.4.

99. This ecclesial interpretation extends into the twentieth century. See Peter Fransen, *Divine Grace and Man* (New York: The New American Library, 1962), 118–21 and Henri Rondet, *The Grace of Christ* (Westminster, MD: Newman Press, 1967), 55.

100. Bernard of Clairvaux, *On the Song of Songs*, vol. III, Sermon 61.2 (Kalamazoo, MI: Cistercian Publications, 1979), 141.

101. Ibid., Sermon 79.1, vol. IV (1980), 137.

102. Ibid., vol. I, Sermon 20.4, p. 149.

103. Barbara Newman explores the unparalleled optimism about human love in the twelfth century, with its concomitant dark side in the form of distrust of sexuality, canon law's taboos about even marital sex, the campaign for clerical celibacy, misogynist satire. "The Mozartian Moment: Reflections on Medieval Mysticism," *Christian Spirituality Bulletin* 3/1 (Spring 1995): 4.

104. Phipps, "The Plight," 82.

105. See "Rethinking Sex and Spirituality: The Song of Songs and Its Readings," by David McLain Carr, *Soundings* 81/3–4 (Fall/Winter, 1998): 413–35.

106. Catalogues in monastic libraries attest to the popularity of the Song. In the twelfth century, the library at Cluny listed fifteen commentaries, including those of Origen and Gregory of Nyssa. Among some seventy manuscripts preserved at Orval, there are seven commentaries on the Song. See Jean Leclercq, *The Love of Learning and the Desire for God* (New York: Fordham University Press, 1961), 106. In all, there is evidence for some thirty commentaries written during the

twelfth century. Some of the more famous Christian commentators on the Song include Origen (d. 254), Gregory of Nyssa (fourth century), Gregory the Great (d. 604), Bede (d. 735), Bernard of Clairvaux (d. 1153), Anselm of Laon (d. 1117), and William of St Thierry (d. 1148). An astute analysis of this commentary tradition can be found in E. Ann Matter's *The Voice of My Beloved: The Song of Songs in Western Medieval Christianity* (Philadelphia: University of Pennsylvania Press, 1990).

107. Beryl Smalley, *Medieval Exegesis of Wisdom Literature* (Atlanta: Scholars Press, 1986), 40.

108. *Love of Learning*, 107–08.

109. W. Phipps, "The Plight," 100.

110. Roland Murphy, "Patristic and Medieval Exegesis—Help or Hindrance?" *The Catholic Biblical Quarterly* 43 (October 1981): 515–16.

111. David McLain Carr, "Rethinking Sex and Spirituality," 414, 432.

112. Constance Fitzgerald asks this question about Carmelite spirituality in "Passion in the Carmelite Tradition: Edith Stein," in *Carmelite Prayer: A Tradition for the 21st Century*, ed. Keith J. Egan (New York/Mahwah, NJ: Paulist Press, 2003), 197, n. 1.

113. For example, see Jon Sobrino, *Spirituality of Liberation: Toward Political Holiness* (Maryknoll, NY: Orbis Books, 1988), 47–48, 70–72.

114. Gustavo Gutierrez, *We Drink From Our Own Wells: The Spiritual Journey of a People* (Maryknoll, NY: Orbis Books, 1984), 60–91.

3. Passion in Hildegard of Bingen

1. William James uses this argument in his classic work on mysticism, *Varieties of Religious Experience* (New York: New American Library, 1958).

2. An alternative interpretation sees Eve as offering humanity one of its greatest gifts—making the choice for knowledge and understanding.

3. Caroline Walker Bynum, *Jesus as Mother: Studies in the Spirituality of the High Middle Ages* (Berkeley: University of California Press, 1982), 139, n. 98. See also Elisabeth Schüssler Fiorenza, "Word, Spirit and Power: Women in Early Christian Communities," in *Women of Spirit*, eds. R. Ruether and E.C. McLaughlin (New York: Simon and

Schuster, 1979); and Rachel Moriarity, "'Playing the Man': The Courage of Christian Martyrs, Translated and Transposed," in *Gender and Christian Religion*, ed. R. N. Swanson, Studies in Church History, 34 (Woodbridge, UK: The Boydell Press, 1998), 1–11. For analyses of women's holiness that go beyond the virago tradition of earliest Christianity, see Barbara Newman, ed., *From Virile Woman to WomanChrist* (Philadelphia: University of Pennsylvania Press, 1995).

4. Ibid., 172. Bynum cites A. Rayez, "Humanité du Christ," *Dictionnaire du Spiritualité* 7.1: cols.1088–90; and I.M. Lewis, *Ecstatic Religion* (Middlesex, UK: Harmondsworth, 1971), 32.

5. Cited in T.J. Jackson Lears, *No Place of Grace: Antimodernism and the Transformation of American Culture, 1880–1920* (New York: Pantheon Books, 1981), 161.

6. In an essay entitled "Religious Thinker," Constant Mews notes that the search for rational analogies to describe Christian doctrine was a characteristic feature of twelfth–century theology. Peter Abelard is a major example of this tendency. In Barbara Newman, ed., *Voice of the Living Light: Hildegard of Bingen and Her World* (Berkeley: University of California Press, 1998), 56, 58.

7. For a life of Hildegard see *The Life of Holy Hildegard*, by the monks Gottfried and Theoderic, trans. Adelgundis Fuhrkotter and James McGrath (Collegeville, MN: The Liturgical Press, 1994). See also Barbara Newman, "'Sibyl of the Rhine': Hildegard's Life and Times," in *Voice of the Living Light*, 1–29; Renate Craine, *Hildegard: Prophet of the Cosmic Christ* (New York: Crossroad, 1997); and Sabina Flanagan, *Hildegard of Bingen: A Visionary Life* (London: Routledge, 1989).

8. A significant collection of Hildegard's work can be found in J.–P. Migne, ed., *Sanctae Hildegardis abbatissae Opera omnia*, in *Patrologiae cursus completus*: series latina 197 (Paris, 1855).

9. See *Hildegard of Bingen: The Book of the Rewards of Life*, trans. Bruce W. Hozeski (New York and Oxford: Oxford University Press, 1994).

10. Hildegard of Bingen, *Holistic Healing*, trans. Manfred Pawlik, Patrick Madigan (Collegeville, MN: The Liturgical Press, 1994).

11. See Barbara Newman, ed., *Hildegard of Bingen: Symphonia* 2nd ed. (Ithaca, NY, and London: Cornell University Press, 1988).

12. See Barbara Newman, *Sister of Wisdom: St. Hildegard's Theology of the Feminine* (Berkeley: University of California Press, 1987), 10–11.

13. See essay by Joan Ferrante, "Correspondent," in Barbara Newman, ed., *Voice of the Living Light*, 91–109.

14. See *The Letters of Hildegard of Bingen*, 2 vols., trans. Joseph L. Baird and Radd K. Ehrman (New York and Oxford: Oxford University Press, 1994 and 1998).

15. Barbara Newman, *Voice of the Living Light*, 64.

16. Ibid., 65.

17. Ibid., 15.

18. Kent Kraft, "The German Visionary: Hildegard of Bingen," in *Medieval Women Writers*, ed. Katharina M. Wilson (Athens: University of Georgia Press, 1984), 115.

19. In the volume, *Hildegard: Prophet of the Cosmic Christ*, Renate Craine includes chapters on "The Way of the Heart" (6: 99–106) and "Love" (9: 143–54).

20. The impact of Hildegard's use of color is visible in the colored renderings of the visions in *Illuminations of Hildegard of Bingen*, ed. Matthew Fox (Santa Fe, NM: Bear & Company, 1995).

21. All references are to *Hildegard of Bingen: Scivias*, The Classics of Western Spirituality, trans. Mother Columba Hart and Jane Bishop (New York/Mahwah, NJ: Paulist Press, 1990).

22. *The Letters*, vol. I, 7. Hildegard connects *viriditas* with moisture (*humor, humiditas*). If the earth did not have moisture or greenness it would crumble like ashes. In the spiritual realm both *viriditas* and *humiditas* are "manifestations of God's power, qualities of the human soul, for 'the grace of God shines like the sun and sends its gifts in various ways; in wisdom, in greenness, in moisture.'" (Letter 85r/b) 195. In the spiritual realm, a lack of moisture causes virtues to become dry as dust (Letter 85r/a), 194.

23. Barbara Newman, "Hildegard of Bingen" video (Washington, DC: The National Cathedral, 1989).

24. *The Letters*, vol. I, 7. See also Letter 101 in vol. II, 16.

25. Letter 38r, *The Letters*, vol. 1, 107.

26. *Scivias*, III.10.4, p. 475; III.10.7, p. 478. Hildegard describes the power of Antichrist as the ability to set the air in motion, bring forth fire and lightnings, raise thunders and hailstorms, uproot mountains, dry up water, and take the greenness from forests. III.11.27, pp. 502–503.

27. Ibid., II.4.2, p. 190.

28. Letter 319, *Hildegardis Bingensis Epistolarum*, Corpus Christianorum, v. 91b (Turnhout, Belgium: Brepols Publishers, 2001), 79.

29. Ibid.

30. The use of marriage imagery to describe mystical experience (known in German as *brautmystik*) increased in the twelfth and thirteenth centuries. Caroline Walker Bynum offers two reasons for this development. The first is a new emphasis on marriage as a sacrament in twelfth–century theology and canon law. Second, many spiritual writers of this period entered the monastery later in life. The new monastic orders preferred to recruit adults so that "the percentage of monks and nuns who had been married before their conversion appears to have become much higher." Therefore the experiences of married love would have been known firsthand. *Jesus as Mother*, 142. Hildegard uses the image of daughter as frequently as she uses that of spouse.

31. See for example Letters 16r, 91r, 106r, and 115r in *The Letters*, vol. I, 66; vol. II, 6, 41, 61.

32. Barbara Newman, *Sister of Wisdom*, 21. Hildegard protests that Mary was never touched by sexual desire (II.6.14), states that physical sex pollutes (II.6.26); and offers a minimal endorsement of marriage for the purpose of procreation alone (III.10.3).

33. Ibid.

34. Letter 344, *Hildegardis Bingensis Epistolarum*.

35. The anti–Semitism visible in this text is an all too present strain in medieval theology and spirituality.

36. Letter 109r, *The Letters*, vol. II, 49. See also Letter 40, I, 110.

37. Ibid., 48.

38. Occasionally Hildegard uses the image of blood, by means of which the Holy Spirit surrounds and warms humans. In other texts, blood symbolizes defilement and slavery to burning fleshly desires (*Scivias* III.7.8). For an extended treatment of the function of blood symbolism in the texts of medieval women mystics, see Caroline Walker Bynum, *Jesus as Mother*, 131, 151f.

39. Letter 91r, *The Letters*, vol. II, 6.

40. Letter 95. Ibid., 11.

41. One scholar sees in this conflict evidence of the perennial struggle in the church between charism and institution. See A.

Fuhrkotter, *Briefsechsel: Nach den altesten Handschriften übersetz und nach Quellen erlautert*, 235–46.

42. Newman, *Sister of Wisdom*, 9.

43. Scholars have investigated the physical causes of visionary experiences. Some attempt to analyze the symptoms in medical categories; other describe them reductively as "hallucinations." An example of the former is Charles Singer, who attributes the visions to migrainous scintillating scotoma. See "The Scientific Views and Visions of Saint Hildegard" in *Studies in the History and Method of Science*, 1–55. Cited in Kraft, "The German Visionary," 119.

44. Letter 103r, *The Letters*, vol. II, 23.

45. Hildegard also presents a God who is impatient with the poor who waste what is given to them out of greed (*Scivias* II.6.91).

46. Rosemary Haughton, *On Trying to Be Human* (Springfield, IL: Templegate, 1966), 137.

47. This term refers to the kidneys or loins, thought to be the seat of the emotions and affections. In the ancient world, the term was used as a synonym for the emotional aspects of the human person.

48. Letter 66r, *The Letters*, vol. I, 146.

49. Barbara Newman argues that toward the end of her life, Hildegard had largely given up on the church's ability to reform itself. In addition to the strong faithful remnant of believers, she saw the aristocracy (her own class) as most able to assist in the reform of the clergy. In "Prophet and Reformer," *Voice of the Living Light*, 89.

50. Letter 149r to Werner, a priest of Kirchheim, *The Letters*, vol. II, 92. Cited in Barbara Newman, "'Sibyl of the Rhine,'" in *Voice of the Living Light*, 20.

51. Letter 16r, *The Letters*, vol. I, 67.

52. Letter 198 to Abbess Elizabeth, *The Letters*, vol. II, 172.

53. For example, Letters 155r, 209r, *The Letters*, vol. II, 100, 191.

54. In the summer of 1163, several Cathars were executed outside Cologne.

55. Hildegard delivered a public sermon against the Cathars at the Cologne Cathedral around 1163 and wrote a short treatise against them—"De Catharis," in *Analecta Sanctae Hildegardis*, ed. Jean–Baptiste Pitra, *Analecta Sacra*, vol. 8. (Monte Cassino, 1882), 348–51.

56. Joan Ferrante analyzes Hildegard's letters in an essay entitled "Correspondent," in Barbara Newman, ed., *Voice of the Living Light*, 91–109.

57. Letter 62, *The Letters*, vol. I, 141.

58. Letter 117, *The Letters*, vol. II, 62.

59. Letter 157, *The Letters*, vol. II, 104.

60. Letter 215r, *The Letters*, vol. II, 196.

61. See Sabina Flanagan, *Hildegard of Bingen*, 180–84.

62. Letter 64, *The Letters*, vol. I, 143–44.

63. Related to this event are Letters, 12, 13 and 13r, *The Letters*, vol. I, 48–52.

64. Ibid., 51.

65. Letter 201r, *The Letters*, vol. II, 181. Margaret Wade Labarge uses this image for the title of her book, *A Small Sound of the Trumpet: Women in Medieval Life* (Boston: Beacon Press, 1986).

66. *Scivias*, 493. The image can be found on p. 491. In her essay, "Prophet and Reformer," Kathryn Kerby–Fulton notes that Hildegard's interest in gynecology and exorcism may explain the graphic detail of this passage but not its savagery. She notes that Hildgard sees corrupt clergy as the forerunners of the Antichrist who "commit a kind of sexual assault on Ecclesia." Gregorian reformers often used the metaphor of rape to describe simony—the practice of buying and selling church offices. In Barbara Newman, ed. *Voice of the Living Light*, 83.

67. Cited in Barbara Newman's essay, "Poet," in *Voice of the Living Light*, 191.

4. Passion in Hadewijch of Brabant

1. Hadewijch is associated geographically with several locations—Antwerp, Brussels, or Brabant. The dialect in which she wrote was Brabant.

2. Courtly love is a name given by medieval scholars to an idealized view of love between a man and a woman. The twelfth–century love poetry of the troubadours in southern France praised the challenges and rewards of the knight who performed feats of bravery for his "lady love." Hallmarks of courtly love included the unattainability of love; the image of the lady on a pedestal, symbol of permanent ideals; the lady's often hard or capricious nature; and erotic, poetic

descriptions of the details of the art of love. A well–known example of loving at a distance is Dante Alighieri's *Vita Nuova*, ed. Mark Musa (Oxford: Oxford University Press, 2000). Barbara Newman discusses a celebrated image of the "Lady " of courtly love—Ulrich von Liechtenstein's (a contemporary of Hadewijch) image of Lady Venus (*Frau Minne*). A crowned lady with a torch in one hand and arrow in the other hovers above her knight riding a horse across the sea to a joust. *God and the Goddesses: Vision, Poetry, and Belief in the Middle Ages* (Philadelphia: University of Pennsylvania Press, 2003), 169. The image can be found on page 170. Newman also notes that the Dutch term for "Lady Love" (*minne*), appears 987 times in Hadewijch's *Poems in Stanzas*, 175.

3. Five manuscripts are extant. Joszef Van Mierlo's critical seven–volume edition of Hadewijch's writings appeared between 1924 and 1952.

4. Mother Columba Hart, *Hadewijch: The Complete Works* (New York/Mahwah, NJ: Paulist Press, 1980), 1. All citations in this chapter are from this translation. The specific reference is indicated in parentheses following the citation.

5. Ibid., xiii.

6. Barbara Newman, *God and the Goddesses*, 171.

7. Bernard McGinn, *The Flowering of Mysticism: Men and Women in the New Mysticism, 1200–1350*, vol. 3 of *The Presence of God: A History of Western Christian Mysticism* (New York: Crossroad, 1998), 199.

8. For analyses of the beguine movement, see Juliette Dor, Lesley Johnson, and Jocelyn Wogan–Browne, eds., *New Trends in Feminine Spirituality: The Holy Women of Liège and Their Impact*, Medieval Women: Texts and Contexts, vol. 2 (Turnhout, Belgium: Brepols Publishers, 1999); Bernard McGinn, *The Flowering of Mysticism*, 199–265; Saskia Murk–Jansen, *Brides in the Desert: The Spirituality of the Beguine*, Traditions of Christian Spirituality Series (Maryknoll, NY: Orbis Books, 1998); Herbert Grundmann, *Religious Movements in the Middle Ages* (Notre Dame, IN: University of Notre Dame Press, 1995), 139–52; Barbara Newman, *From Virile Woman to WomanChrist: Studies in Medieval Religion and Literature* (Philadelphia: University of Pennsylvania Press, 1995), 137–67; Elizabeth Alvilda Petroff, *Body and Soul: Essays on Medieval Women and Mysticism* (Oxford: Oxford University Press, 1994), 51–65; Peter Dinzelbacher, *Mittelalterliche Frauenmystik* (Paderborn: F.

Schoningh, 1993); Joanna Ziegler, "Reality as Imitation: The Role of Religious Imagery Among the Beguines of the Low Countries," in Ulrike Wiethaus, ed., *Maps of Flesh and Light: The Religious Experience of Medival Women Mystics* (Syracuse, NY: Syracuse University Press, 1993), 112–26; Caroline Walker Bynum, *Fragmentation and Redemption: Essays on Gender and the Human Body in Medieval Religion* (New York: Zone Books, 1991); Dennis Devlin, "Feminine Lay Piety in the High Middle Ages: The Beguines," in *Medieval Religious Women*, vol. 1, *Distant Echoes*, eds. John A. Nichols and Lillian Thomas Shank (Kalamzoo, MI: Cistercian Publications, 1984), 183–96; Ernest W. McDonnell, *The Beguines and Beghards in Medieval Culture* (New Brunswick, NJ: Rutgers University Press, 1954).

9. For a treatment of the communal nature of beguine life and the performance aspects of beguine texts, see Mary Suydam, "Beguine Textuality: Sacred Performances," in *Performance and Transformation: New Approaches to Late Medieval Spirituality*, eds. Mary A. Suydam and Joanna E. Ziegler (New York: St. Martin's Press, 1999), 169–210.

10. Alfred Haverkamp notes that by the mid–thirteenth century, about two thousand Beghards and Beguines (the majority) lived in the vicinity of Cologne. *Medieval Germany, 1056–1273*, trans. H. Braun and R. Mortimer, 2nd ed. (Oxford: Oxford University Press, 1992), 318. Cited in Frances Beer, *Women and Mystical Experience in the Middle Ages*, Library of Medieval Women (Suffolk, England: Boydell & Brewer, 1998), 80, n. 4.

11. Jocelyn Wogan–Browne and Marie–Elisabeth Henneau, "Liège: the Medieval 'Woman Question,'" in *New Trends in Feminine Spirituality*, 11–12.

12. Walter Simons, *Cities of Ladies: Beguine Communities in the Medieval Low Countries, 1200–1565*, The Middle Ages Series (Philadelphia: University of Pennsylvania Press, 2001), 142.

13. Margaret Wade Labarge, *A Small Sound of the Trumpet: Women in Medieval Life* (Boston: Beacon Press, 1986), 115.

14. Smaller groups seemed to be the norm in France, while larger groups developed in the Netherlands and Belgium. See Dayton Phillips, *Beguines in Medieval Strasbourg: A Study of the Social Aspects of Beguine Life* (Stanford University dissertation: Edwards Brothers, 1941). Cited in Mary Suydam, "Beguine Textuality," p. 198, n. 6. Examples of beguine architecture can still be seen in Bruges and Amsterdam.

15. Cited in Frank Tobin's Introduction to Mechthild of Magdeburg's *The Flowing Light of the Godhead* (New York/Mahwah, NJ: Paulist Press, 1998), 2.

16. Ibid.

17. Ibid., 3.

18. Hart, *Hadewijch*, 4–5.

19. Barbara Newman, *"La mystique courtoise*: Thirteenth–Century Beguines and the Art of Love," in *From Virile Woman to WomanChrist*, 137–39.

20. Bernard McGinn, *The Flowering of Christian Mysticism*, 169–70.

21. Ria Vanderauwera, "The Brabant Mystic: Hadwijch," in *Medieval Women Writers*, ed. Katharina M. Wilson (Athens: University of Georgia Press, 1984), 186. Hadewijch uses several different terms for love: *Karitate* usually refers to love of neighbor; *lief* refers to the beloved who is either Christ or the soul; *minne*, a word of feminine gender and belonging to the language of courtly love, is used most often. See Hart, *Hadewijch*, 8. Saskia Murk–Jansen discusses the linguistic dimensions of a possible influence of Hadewijch's writing on Eckhart in "Hadewijch and Eckhart: *Amor intellegere est*," in *Meister Eckhart and the Beguine Mystics: Hadewijch of Brabant, Mechthild of Magdeburg and Marguerite Porete*, ed. Bernard McGinn (New York: Continuum, 1994), 17–21.

22. Ibid., 188. Vanderauwera refers here to the work of N. de Paepe, *Hadewijch: Strofische Gedichten* (Ghent, 1967).

23. Newman, *God and the Goddesses*, 175, 177.

24. Bernard McGinn, *The Flowering of Mysticism*, 170. McGinn suggests that *minne* "must be predicated of God, but it also signifies the fundamental reality or power by which all things participate in God and by which they return to him." As used by the women mystics, it is a more phenomenological than a metaphysical term—pointing to a varied range of meanings (171). For further discussion of the meanings of *minne*, see Jessica A. Boon, "Trinitarian Love Mysticism: Ruusbroec, Hadewijch, and the Gendered Experience of the Divine," *Church History* 72/3 (September 2003): 490–91, especially n. 25.

25. Tanis Guest shows how Hadwijch made use of the conventions of the courtly love song: nature opening, tripartition, tornada, rhyme scheme, concatenation, and imagery. *Some Aspects of Hadewijch's*

Poetic Form in the "Strofische Gedichten" (The Hague, 1975). Cited in Vanderauwera, "The Brabant Mystic," 189.

26. Vanderauwera, "The Brabant Mystic," 189.

27. Hart, *Hadewijch*, 19.

28. "The Brabant Mystic," 188. At the end of the thirteenth century there was a vigorous reaction against courtly poetry, and it is supposed that much of it has been lost. Vanderauwera suggests that Hadewijch's poetry survived because of its religious, that is, "safe" content.

29. See Paul Mommaers, "Hadewijch: A Feminist in Conflict," *Louvain Studies* 13 (1988): 69.

30. Mommaers, "Hadewijch: A Feminist in Conflict," 64–65.

31. Ibid., 65.

32. Hart, *Hadewijch*, 11–12.

33. Ibid., 280.

34. Ibid., 281.

35. Origen, *Commentary on the Song of Songs*, cited in *Light From Light: An Anthology of Christian Mysticism*, eds. Louis Dupré and James A. Wiseman, 2nd ed. (New York/Mahwah, NJ: Paulist Press, 2001), 18.

36. Rosemary Haughton, *On Trying to Be Human* (Springfield: Templegate, 1966), 98–99.

37. For an analysis of the links to sexual violence in the texts of medieval women mystics, see Julie B. Miller, "Eroticized Violence in Medieval Women's Mystical Literature: A Call for a Feminist Critique," in *Journal of Feminist Studies in Religion* 15/2 (Fall 1999): 25–49.

38. Joan Chittister offers a contemporary account in *Scarred by Struggle, Transformed by Hope* (Grand Rapids, MI: Eerdmans, 2003).

39. Mary Oliver, *New and Selected Poems* (Boston: Beacon Press, 1992), 10–11.

Conclusion: Back to the Present

1. Clarissa Atkinson includes the controversial fourteenth–century figure, Margery Kempe, in this affective tradition. *Mystic and Pilgrim: The "Book" and the World of Margery Kempe* (Ithaca, NY: Cornell University Press, 1983), 129–30.

2. Ibid., 110.

3. Don E. Saliers, "Beauty and Terror," *Spiritus* 2/2 (Fall 2002): 186.

4. Jonathan Edwards, *Treatise Concerning Religious Affections*, ed. John E. Smith (New Haven: Yale University Press, 1959), 101.

5. Don Saliers, "Beauty and Terror," 189.

6. See Elizabeth A. Dreyer, *Earth Crammed with Heaven: A Spirituality of Everyday Life* (New York/Mahwah, NJ: Paulist Press, 1994); Ronald Rolheiser, *The Holy Longing: The Search for A Christian Spirituality* (New York: Doubleday, 1999); Philip Sheldrake, *Befriending Our Desires* (London: Darton, Longman and Todd, 1994).

7. Rosemary Haughton, *On Trying to Be Human* (Springfield, IL: Templegate, 1966), 106.

8. Miguel de Unamuno, *The Tragic Sense of Life*, trans. J. E. Crawford Flitch (New York: Dover Publications, 1954), 193. Cited in Don Saliers, "Beauty and Terror," 189.

9. Ibid.

Index